AIRBUS A350

NIGEL RICHARDSON

Front cover:
Top: A350-941 OH-LWA of Finnair. (Valentin Hintikka, CC BY 2.0)
Bottom: A350-941 B-LQD of Cathay Pacific Airways. (Author's collection)

Back cover (top to bottom):
A350-1041 A6-XWB of Etihad Airways. (Mark Bess, CC BY-SA 2.0)
A350-941 9V-SMH of Singapore Airlines. (Author's collection)
A350-941 A7-ALA of Qatar Airways. (Gerard van der Schaaf, CC BY 2.0)
A350-1041 G-VJAM of Virgin Atlantic Airways. (HawkeyeUK, CC BY-SA 2.0)
A350-1041 G-XWBH of British Airways. (British Airways)

First published 2025

Amberley Publishing
The Hill, Stroud,
Gloucestershire, GL5 4EP

www.amberley-books.com

Copyright © Nigel Richardson, 2025

The right of Nigel Richardson to be identified as the Author
of this work has been asserted in accordance with the
Copyright, Designs and Patents Act 1988.

All rights reserved. No part of this book may be reprinted
or reproduced or utilised in any form or by any electronic,
mechanical or other means, now known or hereafter invented,
including photocopying and recording, or in any information
storage or retrieval system, without the permission in writing
from the Publishers.

ISBN: 978 1 3981 2413 4 (print)
ISBN: 978 1 3981 2414 1 (ebook)

British Library Cataloguing in Publication Data.
A catalogue record for this book is available from the British Library.

Typeset in 10pt on 13pt Celeste.
Typesetting by SJmagic DESIGN SERVICES, India.
Printed in the UK.

Appointed GPSR EU Representative: Easy Access System Europe Oü, 16879218
Address: Mustamäe tee 50, 10621, Tallinn, Estonia
Contact Details: gpsr.requests@easproject.com, +358 40 500 3575

Contents

	Acknowledgements	4
	Introduction	5
Chapter 1	Design and Development of the Airbus A350	7
Chapter 2	Building the Airbus A350	23
Chapter 3	Airbus A350-900: Into Service	34
Chapter 4	Airbus A350-1000	70
Chapter 5	Airbus A350 Enhancements, Other Variants and Potential Developments	88
	Appendix: Airbus A350 Technical Specifications	96

Acknowledgements

I am especially grateful to Nicolas Fanchin, AudioVisual Libraries & Distribution Specialist for Airbus, who kindly helped source and arrange permission for the use of a large selection of Airbus-owned images in the book. My sincere thanks to the following organisations for their kind co-operation and permission to use some of their images: Airbus, British Airways, Air India, Cathay Pacific Airways, Edelweiss Air, Virgin Atlantic Airways, Finnair, Emirates, Iberia and Qantas. I would like to acknowledge and thank the following photographers for kindly allowing me to include their images in the book either directly or via Creative Commons: 4300streetcar, Jean-Baptiste Accariez, Aero Pixels, Dylan Agbagni, Md Shaifuzzaman Ayon, Bahnfrend, Mark Bess, Richard Blata, Alexis Boidron, Mike Burdett, Steven Byles, Olivier Cabaret, Pablo Cabellos, Rafael Luiz Canossa, Arthur Caudrelier, M. Chainey, Charles, Shaun Connor, Colin Cooke, Rémi Dallot, M Radzi Desa, Don-vip, Alexandre Doumenjou, Laurent Errera, Hervé Goussé, Gyrostat, Steven He, Julian Herzog, Valentin Hintikka, Mitchul Hope, ILA-boy, Kiefer, Frederic Lancelot, Bengt Lange, ltdccba, MarcelX42, Philippe Masclet, Melv_L-MACASR, Joao Carlos Medau, Adam Moreira, N509FZ, Pascal Pigeyre, Sylvain Ramadier, J. V. Reymondon, Bene Riobó, Lars Rohde, Eric Salard, Gerard van der Schaaf, Juke Schweizer, Semduvidas1, Simply Aviation, SuFlyer, John Taggart, Artem Tchaikovski, Alan Wilson, wiltshirespotter, Windmemories and Anna Zvereva. Many thanks to my wife, Gill, for carefully proofreading each chapter of the book. Finally, my thanks to Alison Flowers from Amberley Publishing for her interest in the book, support and advice.

Note

Specific factual content in this book is for information only and should not be used for operational purposes. The information and data presented is believed to be accurate up to August 2025.

Introduction

In the early 1960s Europe's fragmented aviation industry faced an uphill challenge in competition with major North American companies, such as Boeing, Douglas and Lockheed, if it was to become a leader in commercial aviation. Although some European countries had managed to develop successful aircraft, such as the de Havilland Comet, Sud Aviation Caravelle, Hawker Siddeley Trident and Vickers VC10, Europe's internal market was too small and competitive to sustain many different companies. The development of Concorde as a result of collaboration between France and the UK was insufficient to counter the dominance of America in the aerospace industry.

In 1967, France, Germany and the United Kingdom decided to combine their expertise and industrial capacity and design a common wide-body airliner, the A300, to compete with the Americans. By 1969 the British government had withdrawn from its participation in the venture, while the French and German governments signed an agreement to proceed with the building of the aircraft. Airbus Industrie was formally established the following year and the A300 project was launched. Spain joined the consortium in 1971 with manufacturer Construcciones Aeronáuticas S.A. (CASA) acquiring a 4.2 per cent share of the business, leaving Aérospatiale (a merger between two French companies: Sud-Aviation and Nord Aviation) and Deutsche Airbus (a joint venture between Messerschmitt-Bölkow-Blohm and VFW-Fokker) each with shares of 47.9 per cent. The Airbus A300B made its maiden flight from Toulouse in October 1972 and entered into service with Air France on 23 May 1974. Through collaboration with British Aerospace, the UK became an Airbus partner in 1979, acquiring a 20 per cent share.

Airbus' second aircraft type, the A310, first began commercial operations with Lufthansa in 1983. Four years later Airbus' first narrow-body airliner, the A320, made its first flight, pioneering the use of digital fly-by-wire technology and side-stick flight controls in airliners. During the 1990s Airbus extended its range of aircraft, including a diversification of the A320 family with the A318, A319 and A321, and the introduction of two long-haul airliners, the A330 and A340. Airbus worked hard over a thirty-year period to develop aircraft that could compete with Boeing, expanding its range from one aircraft type with no market share to seven new airliners which had attracted almost 1,700 orders. In April 2005 the world's largest airliner, the Airbus A380, took to the skies for the first time as Airbus set its sights on a larger target, competing with the Boeing 747.

Today Airbus is Europe's leading aerospace company and Boeing's main competitor. Although Boeing initially held the leading position in the commercial aviation market, Airbus has gradually increased its market share. The Boeing-Airbus rivalry has generated a series of competitive moves: in the early 2000s Airbus introduced the A330 and A340 as alternatives to the Boeing 767 and 777, while the major commercial success of the Boeing 747, as a result of its excellent durability, high passenger capacity and cost efficiency which revolutionised global air travel in the 1970s, caused Airbus to respond by developing the A380 in an attempt to break the dominance held by Boeing in the high-capacity aircraft market segment. Conversely, Boeing developed the 737MAX as a relatively fast and cost-efficient way of competing with the Airbus A320neo (new engine option) family, which offered superior fuel efficiency to Boeing's 737 NG series.

In April 2004 Boeing launched the 787 Dreamliner (initially called the 7E7 project). The company had decided to develop a new twin-engine aircraft capable of carrying 200–300 passengers on point-to-point routes up to 8,500 nautical miles (nm) as a replacement for its 767. The 787 was designed to be approximately 20 per cent more efficient than the 767 through the use of lighter-weight carbon-fibre composites in the fuselage and wing construction, new engines which were more fuel efficient, greater use of electrical systems, and aerodynamic improvements, including raked wingtips to reduce drag. The Boeing 787 made its first flight in December 2009, by which time it had generated 851 orders. It was the fastest-selling wide-body airliner in history. By the end of 2024 there had been 1,957 orders, of which 1,161 aircraft had been delivered.

Airbus needed a response to the launch of the Boeing 787; however, its initial reaction appeared to be somewhat sluggish. Airbus' engineers had doubts about the performance of the 787 as claimed by Boeing and, at the time, Airbus was stretched, both financially and by the availability of engineering resources due to the technical challenges posed by the A380 programme and the early stages of the A400M programme, which resulted in a general reluctance to begin a third major aircraft development.

Nevertheless, in 2004, Airbus began to work on a lighter and improved version of the A330, designated the A330-200 Lite. It received little customer interest. In 2005 Airbus launched the A350-800/-900, a new aircraft with fuel-efficient engines and composite wings but which still retained a strong resemblance to the A330. Despite generating orders from aircraft lease companies and several airlines, the overall reaction to the initial A350 proposals was lukewarm.

The A350 programme went through five iterations before a completely redesigned, long-range, wide-body, twin-engine airliner was announced at the Farnborough Airshow in July 2006. It was designated the Airbus A350XWB (Extra Wide Body).

This book tells the story of the A350 from its evolution, design, development and construction up to its entry into commercial service. It provides an overview of the A350 in service with major airlines, as well as describing the modifications and improvements that have been made to the original design, including the emergence of several additional variants, and the potential evolution of the aircraft in the future.

CHAPTER 1

Design and Development of the Airbus A350

The development of the Airbus A350 began in 2004 when Airbus was considering a modernisation of the A330, to be called the A330-200 Lite, in response to Boeing's announcement regarding a new aircraft development – the 7E7 (later designated the 787 Dreamliner) – in January 2003. The A330-200 Lite was due to be revealed at the 2004 Farnborough Airshow but it didn't happen. Several months later the CEO of Airbus held a private meeting with major prospective Airbus customers at which he provided details of the new aircraft project. It was very much a low-cost upgrade of its tried and tested A330, with a standard Aluminium-Lithium (Al-Li) A330 fuselage structure and cross-section, although the new design did feature an increasing use of composite materials and manufacturing technologies and was to be powered by fuel-efficient Rolls-Royce Trent or General Electric GEnx engines. In light of the disappointing response from prospective customers to its proposals, Airbus announced that it would commit 4 billion Euros to the design of a brand-new airliner. In December 2004, the major shareholders of Airbus (the European Aeronautic Defence and Space Company (EADS) board and the BAe Systems board) gave approval for Airbus to offer a new aircraft project, designated the A350, with an anticipated entry into service date of 2010.

Initial details of the Airbus A350 were released at the Paris Airshow in June 2005, succeeded by the industrial launch of the project in October 2005. The general design was a twin-engine wide-body jet which had a strong resemblance to the A330. It had an Al-Li fuselage structure with a redesigned wing and horizontal tail plane, mostly constructed from carbon fibre-reinforced polymer (CFRP), new landing gear and an upgraded flight deck. A preliminary contract was signed with General Electric to exclusively develop and supply a new generation engine for the A350, the GEnx-72A1 variant, which would contribute to significant improvements in fuel efficiency. Airbus offered two versions of the new aircraft: the A350-800, which was capable of flying 8,800 nm with a typical passenger load of 253 in a three-class seating configuration, and the longer A350-900, which could accommodate 300 passengers in a three-class configuration and had a range of 7,500 nm. By the end of 2005 Airbus had received 170 orders and commitments from thirteen customers for the planned new airliner, including Qatar Airways (sixty), US Airways (twenty), Air Europa (ten), TAM (eight), Bangkok Airways (six), US airliner leasing company International Lease Finance Corporation (ILFC) (twelve), Kuwaiti leasing group Alafco (twelve) and GE Capital Aviation Services (GECAS) (ten).

In March 2006 Airbus came up against severe criticism from various aircraft lease companies and major airlines over the proposed A350. The CEO of Singapore Airlines felt that after investing time in the design of a new wing, tailplane and cockpit, Airbus should have designed a new fuselage, while the CEO of ILFC described the A350 project as 'a band-aid reaction to the Boeing 787'. The overall consensus was for a more radical approach to the design of this new-generation aircraft. The response from Airbus was to return to the drawing board and consider A350 improvements to meet customer airlines' expectations.

Four months later Airbus announced a new, completely redesigned aircraft at the Farnborough Airshow. It was given a new designation, the A350XWB (Extra Wide Body). The industrial launch followed in December 2006. The new aircraft design featured a wider fuselage cross-section than the A330 (5.96 m (235 in) wide compared with 5.64 m (222 in) of the A330), hence the use of XWB, and a construction based on the extensive use of CFRP and other new materials (initially calculated to be 45 per cent composites and 55 per cent metal). The fuselage of the A350XWB was slightly wider than that of the Boeing 787 but smaller than that of the Boeing 777, its two main competitors. The wider fuselage allowed for seating arrangements ranging from a six-abreast (2+2+2) First Class section, an eight-abreast (2-4-2) Premium Economy section, up to a ten-abreast high-density seating configuration for a maximum capacity of 400–480 passengers, depending on the variant.

There were to be three variants of the A350XWB: a baseline A350-900 with a length of 66.8 m (219 ft 2 in), seating for up to 315 passengers, and a range of 8,300 nm (15,400 km); a shortened A350-800 with a length of 60.5 m (198 ft 6 in), seating for 270 passengers, and a range up to 8,500 nm (15,750 km); and a stretched A350-1000 with a length of 73.8 m (247 ft 1 in), seating for up to 370 passengers, and a range of 8,300 nm (15,400 km). The aircraft was to be powered by new Rolls-Royce XWB engines, developed from the Trent 1000 engine. General Electric, who had previously been selected as the exclusive supplier of GEnx engines for the original A350, showed little interest in being involved with the A350XWB project and was not prepared to develop a more powerful variant of the GEnx-72A1 engine to meet the thrust requirements for the A350-1000. The A350XWB was to use a fly-by-wire flight-control system similar to that originally developed for the A320 in 1987 but which has been enhanced following design improvements and the evolution of the system on subsequent Airbus aircraft types, especially the A380.

Airbus' commitment to the A350XWB came at a time when the company was facing costly delays to the A380 and A400M programmes and financial resources were seriously stretched. Nonetheless, EADS and the Airbus board decided to proceed with the A350XWB, funded out of cash flow, despite an increase in the estimated development costs from 5.5 billion Euros to approximately 9.7 billion Euros as a consequence of the complete redesign of the aircraft. Delivery of the new aircraft to customers was to be phased; the first A350-900 scheduled for mid-2013, followed by the A350-800 in 2014 and the A350-1000 in 2015.

Finnair was the first airline to order the A350XWB, confirming a firm order for eleven A350-900 aircraft (plus eight options) in March 2007. The order represented a conversion of the carrier's original order for the earlier version of the A350. In June 2007 Singapore Airlines signed a contract for the purchase of twenty A350-900XWBs, firming up an expression of intent submitted in July 2006. Renegotiations were also held with other

An initial design of the Airbus A350 based on the Airbus A330. (Airbus)

A model of the Airbus A350XWB on display at the Berlin Air Show in 2008. (ILA-boy, CC BY-SA 4.0)

existing order holders, including Qatar Airways, which announced a $16 billion order for eighty A350XWBs (including twenty A350-800s, forty A350-900s and twenty A350-1000s) at the Paris Airshow in June 2007, replacing its original plans to purchase sixty A350s. Other airlines to place substantial orders during 2007 included Emirates for seventy aircraft (fifty A350-900s and twenty A350-1000s) plus fifty options, US Airways for eighteen A350-800s and four A350-900s (replacing an earlier commitment for twenty of the original A350), representing the first ever order for the A350XWB from a US airline, Russian carrier Aeroflot for eighteen A350-800s and four A350-900s, and TAP Portugal with an order for twelve A350XWBs plus three options. Within a year of its launch, the A350XWB had secured 294 orders.

The first flight of the A350-900 was initially planned for mid-2012, with entry into service in mid-2013. However, in June 2011 both dates were put back six months, and further delays were announced in November 2011, with the planned first flight pushed back to early 2013. Revisions to the schedule were largely due to supply chain problems and the delayed production of CFRP composites, detailed components and sub-assemblies by partners in Europe and the United States. The A350XWB supply chain involved fifty-five suppliers and 125 work packages and was designed to ensure low manufacturing and assembly costs by outsourcing a large proportion of the financial risk of development to the Airbus suppliers.

The first forward fuselage section for the static test airframe (MSN5000) was delivered from the Airbus factory in Saint-Nazaire, France, in December 2011. Final assembly of the first A350 airframe, to be used for the static structural tests, began on the final assembly line at Toulouse in early April 2012 when the front and centre fuselage sections were joined up. The aft fuselage section came from Hamburg, Germany, in late April. However, a manufacturing problem at Airbus' wing production facility at Broughton, UK, led to further delays. Problems involving software used to control a robotic machine which drilled holes for attaching composite wing panels to the underlying structure delayed delivery of the first A350XWB wing to Toulouse until September 2012. Consequently, in July 2012, Airbus announced that the first flight would be delayed until mid-2013 and the entry into service date was put back until the second half of 2014. The delays cost Airbus a reported 124 million Euros in penalty payments to customers. Assembly of MSN5000 was completed in late October 2012 and the test airframe was finally rolled out in November.

Ground Testing of the A350XWB

Prior to the maiden flight of the first A350 test aircraft, thousands of hours of testing on the ground were undertaken. Airbus altered its supply strategy for the A350, choosing to outsource the design, development and production of major subsystems of the aircraft to suppliers. In order to achieve security for the new arrangements, Airbus introduced a new, risk-sharing supplier contract, which included three main aspects of procurement policy: (1) the allocation of comprehensive and integrated work packages to suppliers; (2) early involvement of suppliers in the process; (3) closer collaboration with suppliers. The New Supplier Policy gave suppliers more autonomy for the development and certification testing of work packages (i.e. new systems and components) for the aircraft.

Suppliers began the process by developing and testing prototype equipment for new technologies that were to be introduced on the aircraft. This was followed by component testing to demonstrate the performance and reliability of each component (and/or software) as part of so-called 'qualification testing'. Suppliers responsible for a complete system, or part of one, then carried out pre-integration testing, which involved verifying the interface of their system with other systems using software models provided by Airbus. Although the supplier performed these tests, they were carried out in collaboration with Airbus' engineers who provided support and advice and ensured that the appropriate testing was undertaken. Refinement and completion of pre-integration testing allowed the component/system in its initial standard (S0) to be delivered to Airbus.

The next stage involved integration testing at Airbus' Flight and Integration Test Centre in Toulouse using Functional Integration Benches to test the systems, components and/or software delivered from suppliers with the systems around it. The benches included hardware for the systems being tested and models for absent systems still to be provided by suppliers and were used to test key functions on the aircraft and the interfaces between systems. For example, the 'Control and Guidance' integration bench was used to test the complete flight control and autopilot system. Hardware (and software) was developed and updated as the testing progressed, with different standards reflecting the level of development. S0 was the initial standard arising from the pre-integration testing; S1 was the standard for final assembly testing; S2 was the standard suitable for the first flight; and S3 was the standard for the aircraft's entry into service.

Integration testing also involved the use of 'zero' ground test rigs, which provided a complete representation of the systems to be installed on the aircraft. The high-lift rig at Bremen, Germany, comprised a complete left-hand 'wing' including all the systems to be installed on the first test aircraft, with the aircraft structure replaced by a steel structure, which allowed the high-lift system to be installed and operated. The rig was used to test the operation of the mechanical drive-shafts, actuators and linkages effective in deploying the flap and slat systems, together with safety tests and the simulation of extreme conditions which would be too dangerous to test in flight, such as the failure of drive-shafts and linkages. A landing gear rig, located at BAE Systems, Filton, UK, consisting of a complete landing gear system, was used to test the full operation of the landing gear, including the emergency lowering of the gear by gravity. A cabin rig built in Hamburg, Germany, consisting of a series of functional integration benches linked to a mock-up of the full A350XWB fuselage, was used to perform a series of virtual cabin flights to test all the cabin systems prior to the first flight of the second development aircraft (MSN002). MSN002 was to be fitted with the full interior, including the air circulation system, air-conditioning system, galleys, in-flight entertainment system and the toilets.

Two complete A350XWB cockpit simulators connected to actual aircraft flight computers were used as integration simulators from early 2012 to test the interface between all the systems and the computers. Each element had been previously tested separately; the integrated tests confirmed that they all worked together as designed. Subsequent operational testing allowed flight crews to complete virtual first flights, allowing the response of the aircraft and its systems to simulated problems scenarios, such as the loss of electrical power, to be tested and analysed.

At Toulouse, a large test rig known as the 'Iron Bird' was constructed from 170 tonnes of steel scaffolding. It was a large framework, fashioned in the skeletal shape of the aircraft, within which major working components identical to those used on the first test aircraft were installed in their relative location within the actual airframe. The components included complete hydraulic, electrical and flight control systems, from power generators (i.e. aircraft hydraulic pumps and electrical generators) through to power users (e.g. flight control actuators, landing gear actuators). The Iron Bird was used initially for integration testing of most of the aircraft's systems where components are readily accessible. Subsequent connection of the cockpit integration simulator to the Iron Bird in early 2013 created the so-called 'aircraft zero', where a pilot could 'fly' the Iron Bird through a flight deck simulator. Aircraft zero was a valuable resource for flight crews since it represented a flying A350XWB, which allowed many tests to be completed using simulated scenarios, including a virtual first flight, prior to the maiden flight of the actual aircraft.

By the beginning of June 2013, 12,260 hours of testing had been carried out using the test rigs and this continued alongside that being undertaken by the five test aircraft to investigate specific issues that arose during the flight test programme. Use of the Iron Bird continued beyond aircraft certification to test system enhancements before introduction on in-service aircraft.

Structural Static Testing

Static load testing is completed to investigate the structural integrity of the airframe and validate the design of the aircraft. The tests simulate the aerodynamic loads and forces to which the aircraft will be subjected during various stages of the flight cycle and analyse the response of the aircraft's structure. They typically involve maximum bending of the wings, aileron and spoiler functional testing during wing bend and fuselage pressure tests. Subsequent certification tests push the airframe beyond its typical operational flight envelope to ensure that it is strong enough to withstand loads associated with abnormal and extreme conditions which are well in excess of those experienced during normal airline operations.

The A350XWB static test airframe (MSN5000), which was the first to be built on the new final assembly line at Toulouse, was integrated into a test rig within a specialist static test hall at Toulouse in December 2012. It was fitted with 12,000 sensors for measuring and monitoring the strains induced into the airframe, 240 jacks/loading lines which are used to induce structural loads, and almost 60 km of hydraulic pipes and 19 km of cables. The first major tests, completed in December 2013, were of the x1.25 limit load and the x1.5 ultimate load of the aircraft's fuselage and wing. The ultimate load wing test involved deflecting the wing in excess of 5 m to simulate the ultimate load beyond or at which the wing is expected to fail. The wing was subjected to loads 1.5 times greater than the expected G load that the aircraft would ever experience in its service life. The ultimate load test of the fuselage involved pressurising the fuselage to over 150 per cent of its normal operating condition.

Fatigue testing explores how the aircraft's structure responds to repeated flight cycles. The data obtained provides precise information on structural behaviour during the aircraft's lifetime and is used to inform the timing and methods of inspection to be

Above: The A350XWB test rig called 'Iron Bird' at Toulouse, France. (Airbus)

Below: The full-scale static test rig shown here conducting the ultimate load wing test. (Hervé Goussé/Airbus)

implemented for the identification of potential areas of inadequate strength and fatigue while the aircraft is in service. In a dynamic test rig the airframe was repeatedly loaded and unloaded using hydraulic jacks to simulate vibrations, twists and distortions experienced during multiple flight cycles. In addition to the static test airframe, full-scale, simulated flight fatigue testing was also carried out on the centre section of the fuselage and both wings at Erding in Germany, on the nose fuselage section at Toulouse and on the rear fuselage section at Hamburg. The A350 fatigue certification tests covered a simulated period equivalent to three times the aircraft's design lifetime to ensure it encompassed a large safety window for potential fatigue.

Left: Airbus A380-800 engine flying test bed with a Rolls-Royce Trent XWB-84 engine mounted on the inner port-side pylon (with a blue nacelle). (Laurent Errera, CC BY-SA 2.0)

Below: The A350XWB static test airframe (MSN5000) after the completion of testing in December 2014. (Gyrostat, CC-BY-SA 4.0)

Testing the Rolls-Royce Trent XWB-84 Engine

The Rolls-Royce Trent XWB-84 test campaign began in June 2010, initially involving the use of a static test-bed. Over 1,500 hours of ground testing were completed, including endurance running, icing and simulated altitude performance, before flight testing began on 18 February 2012 with the engine fitted to Airbus' dedicated Airbus A380 flying test-bed. A 175-hour flight test programme included different power settings up to full power, a range of speeds up to Mach 0.9, altitude testing up to 43,000 ft and engine performance during go-around and rejected take-off scenarios. Flight testing was also conducted in extreme environmental conditions: hot weather testing at Al Ain in the United Arab Emirates, extreme low temperature trials (as low as -23 degrees Centigrade) at Iqaluit, Canada, and altitude and crosswind tests in the USA. The Trent XWB-84 engine received Engine Type Certification from the European Aviation Safety Agency in February 2013 following almost three years of certification testing, which involved eleven engines running for more than 3,100 hours.

Preparation for the First Flight

Final assembly of the first flyable test aircraft, MSN001, began at Toulouse in October 2012. The front fuselage section was delivered in July 2012 followed by the centre and aft fuselage sections in October. The flight deck was powered up in late July following the initial application of electrical power to the front fuselage section. The wings were delivered from the Airbus wing assembly site in Broughton, North Wales, in September 2012. Since the fuselage sections and wings arrive on the final assembly line with systems already installed, once the fuselage sections have been mated and the wings, horizontal and vertical stabilisers attached, the electrical systems can be connected and powered on for the first time. MSN001 was rolled out of the main assembly hall in early December 2012. During early 2013 it underwent comprehensive functional testing of the electrical, hydraulic and fuel systems and initial testing of the flight control surfaces. By late February the aircraft was structurally complete following the installation of the winglets, various fuselage fairings and the main landing gear doors. Further indoor and outdoor testing included: stability tests of movable elements, such as the flaps, elevators, ailerons, rudder and spoilers; lowering and retraction of the landing gear; fuel tank testing (including seals, levels, fuel flow and internal fuel transfer functioning); pressure testing of the fuselage and testing of the aircraft's radio equipment and systems. The engines were installed at the end of March 2013 before the aircraft entered the paint shop at the beginning of May.

As part of the preparations for the maiden flight, the Rolls-Royce XWB engines on MSN001 were powered up for the first time on 2 June 2013 after the aircraft's auxiliary power unit (APU) had been started. Engine run-up tests followed and on 9 June the aircraft began low speed taxi trials and braking tests at various speeds on the runway at Toulouse.

The maiden flight of the first A350-900, F-WXWB (MSN001), was on 14 June 2013 from Toulouse-Blagnac Airport. The duration of the flight was 4 hr 5 min, during which the aircraft flew a racetrack pattern up to 25,000 ft over south-west France before returning to Toulouse. The aircraft remained at 10,000 ft for the first 30 minutes of the flight, maintaining a speed of approximately 200 knots with the landing gear extended. Once the initial handling checks were complete, the landing gear was retracted and the aircraft climbed to an initial cruising altitude of 13,000 ft, before climbing to 25,000 ft, accelerating to 490 knots and undertaking additional handling trials for the final hour of the flight. The aircraft was initially flown under Direct flight control law until validation of the flap configurations had been completed, at which stage the flight computers were engaged and Normal flight control law implemented.

The subsequent twelve months saw the test fleet increase to five development aircraft; the first flight of F-WZGG (MSN003) taking place on 14 October 2013, those of F-WWCF (MSN002) and F-WZNW (MSN004) on 26 February 2014 and that of the fifth and final test aircraft, F-WWYB (MSN005), on 20 June 2014. The first two development aircraft (MSN001 and MSN003) were fitted with an extensive array of flight test instrumentation and monitoring equipment. MSN002 had a medium-level test instrumentation fit while both MSN004 and MSN005 were only lightly instrumented. The roles of each development aircraft in the flight test and certification programme are detailed below.

MSN001/ F-WXWB	Initial handling qualities; flight envelope, systems and engine testing; natural icing; strong crosswind testing in Keflavik, Iceland.
MSN002/ F-WWCF	Performance and environmental trials, including hot weather trials in Al Ain, United Arab Emirates and extreme hot (up to 45 degrees Centigrade) and cold weather (as low as -40 degrees Centigrade) testing at the McKinley Climatic Laboratory, Eglin Air Force Base, Florida; full cabin installation to test cabin systems for cabin development and cabin certification testing; early long-range flights.
MSN003/ F-WZGG	Demonstration and validation of the engines; APU and systems functionality including under extreme conditions during take-off and landing; performance trials under cold weather conditions in Iqaluit, Canada and at high altitude at Cochabamba and La Paz, Bolivia.
MSN004/ F-WZNW	Avionics development and certification; testing of the cockpit head-up-display; water ingestion testing of the engines; extreme crosswind testing at Clermont-Ferrand Auvergne Airport in France; external noise and lighting-strike tests; training the first customer pilots and maintenance teams.
MSN005/ F-WWYB	The second development aircraft fitted with a full passenger cabin interior for cabin operability testing and training; route proving; extended-range twin operations (ETOPS) validation.

The first Airbus A350-900, F-WXWB (MSN001), takes off on its maiden flight from Toulouse-Blagnac Airport on 14 June 2013. (Laurent Errera, CC BY-SA 2.0)

Right: Airbus A350-900 F-WXWB (MSN001) taxiing in after the completion of its first flight. (Don-vip, CC BY-SA 3.0)

Below: Airbus A350-900 test aircraft F-WZGG (MSN003). This aircraft made its first flight on 14 October 2013. (Gyrostat, CC-BY-SA 4.0)

Above: The third A350-900 test aircraft to fly was F-WWCF (MSN002). (Julian Herzog, CC BY 4.0)

Left: A350-900 test aircraft MSN002 displaying at the Paris Air Show in June 2015. (Eric Salard, CC BY-SA 2.0)

Below: The fourth A350-900 test aircraft, F-WZNW (MSN004), first flew on 26 February 2014. (wiltshirespotter, CC BY-SA 2.0)

Above: The final A350-900 test aircraft, F-WWYB (MSN005), was fitted with a full passenger cabin interior and completed route proving trials involving short-, medium- and long-haul flights during a twenty-day world tour. (Kiefer, CC BY-SA 2.0)

Below: Flight test instrumentation and monitoring equipment on board the fifth test aircraft (MSN005). This aircraft was only lightly instrumented. (Joao Carlos Medau, CC BY-SA 2.0)

In July/August 2014, the fifth development aircraft (MSN005) successfully completed route proving trials involving short-, medium- and long-haul flights during a twenty-day world tour. The technical route involved four trips, each starting from Toulouse. The first trip was to Iqaluit, Canada, returning via Frankfurt. The second trip went to Asia, during which time it operated multiple flights between Hong Kong and Singapore. The third trip included flights between Johannesburg and Sydney and Auckland and Santiago de Chile, which demonstrated the capability of the aircraft to fly ultra-long-haul routes and extended-range twin-engine operations (ETOPS). The fourth and final trip went via Doha to

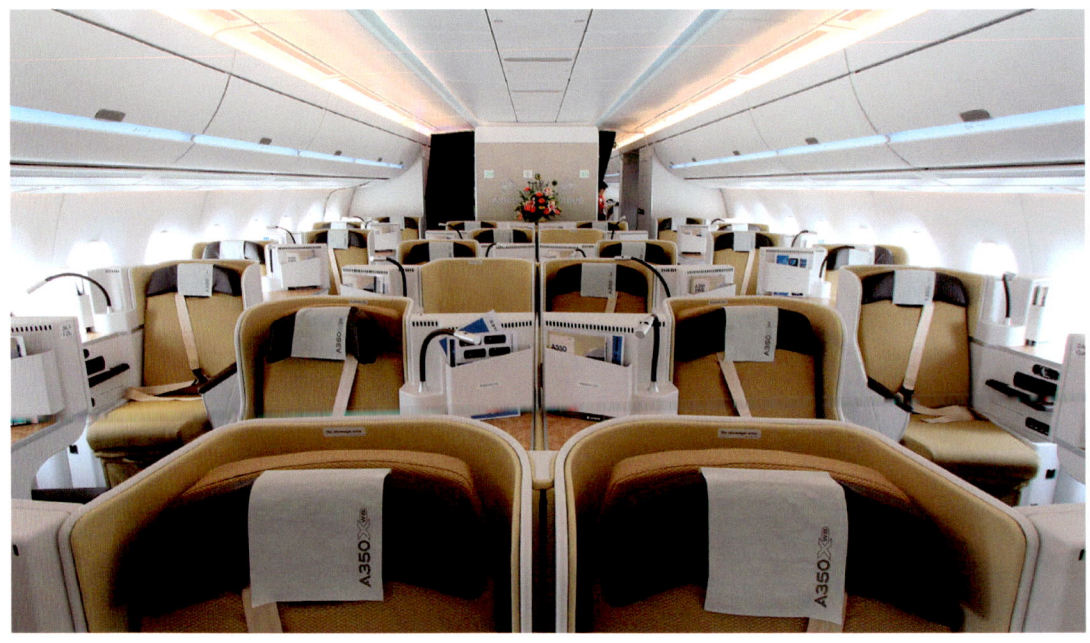

Above: The Business Class section of the full cabin, which was installed on test aircraft MSN002 to test cabin systems and for cabin certification testing. (M. Radzi Desa)

Left: The Economy Class section of the cabin installed on test aircraft MSN002. (Joao Carlos Medau, CC BY 2.0)

Perth, back to Doha, then on to Moscow and Helsinki, before returning to Toulouse. During the tour the aircraft flew approximately 81,700 nm (151,300 km) and 180 flight hours, with each flight performed on schedule. The flights were operated by flight crews from Airbus and by launch customer Qatar Airways on the route from Doha to Perth, Moscow and Helsinki. Several legs were flown by Airworthiness Authority pilots from EASA as part of the Type Certification process.

The fifteen-month flight test and certification programme, which involved more than 2,600 flight test hours, resulted in the A350-900 receiving Type Certification from the European Aviation Safety Agency (EASA) on 30 September 2014. U.S. Federal Aviation Administration (FAA) safety approval was gained two months later, on 13 November.

Airbus launched the A330-800neo and A330-900neo as the next evolution of its reliable and versatile A330 family at the Farnborough Airshow in July 2014, signalling the end for the A350-800, which was the shorter variant of the A350 family and had been offered to airlines as providing slightly greater range and increased efficiency but with approximately forty-five less seats than the A350-900. The A350-800 was seen as a potential competitor to the Boeing 787-8 and 787-9 and by 2008 it had received over 180 orders. The A350-800 gradually became a less attractive option, being perceived as an expensive A330-300 with similar estimated operating costs to the larger A350-900. As the A350 development costs increased, the -900 and -1000 variants became more important to Airbus because the larger aircraft were more profitable. In order to have an aircraft which could compete against the Boeing 787, Airbus decided to proceed with a re-engined A330. Following its launch, a former Airbus CEO claimed that the A330neo (new engine option) was a cheaper, more efficient option than the A350-800 and that customers would convert existing A350-800 orders to either the A350-900 or the A330neo. As predicted, most airlines switched away from the -800, leaving Airbus with no option other than to cancel the A350-800 programme.

A350-900 MSN003 undertaking cold weather trials in Iqaluit, Canada. (Hervé Goussé/Airbus)

Above: Test aircraft MSN003 landing at Iqaluit, Canada. (Hervé Goussé/Airbus)

Left: A350-900 MSN002 undergoing extreme cold weather testing at McKinley Climatic Laboratory, Florida, where it was subject to temperatures as low as minus 40 degrees Centigrade. (Sylvain Ramadier/Airbus)

A350-900 MSN004 successfully undertakes water ingestion tests at Istres Air Base, France. (Jean-Baptiste Accariez/Airbus)

Chapter 2

Building the Airbus A350

As with all the Airbus family of commercial aircraft, the construction of the A350 is a large, pan-European project. Major structural sections of the aircraft are built at Airbus facilities in France, Germany, Spain and the United Kingdom. In addition, there is an extensive international supplier network, producing components and parts for delivery to the main Airbus factories and subsequent integration into the various sub-assemblies. Construction of the sub-assemblies is assigned to specific facilities with the required expertise and manufacturing equipment and techniques.

In France, the Airbus plant at Saint-Nazaire assembles and equips the nose fuselage section, delivered from Hamburg, and mates it with the centre fuselage section prior to testing. The factory at Nantes specialises in the manufacture and assembly of the centre wing box, while the Saint-Eloi site assembles the engine pylons.

Airbus' Hamburg factory in Germany has responsibility for the assembly and installation of flight relevant equipment in the rear and forward fuselage sections, before the latter is transported to Saint-Nazaire. The Stade facility in Germany manufactures the upper and lower shells of the rear fuselage section, and assembles, equips and tests the vertical stabiliser. The wings are delivered from Broughton (UK) to Bremen in Germany for fitting out, which includes installation of the flight control surfaces and high lift devices, hydraulic lines and electric cables.

The Airbus site at Illescas in Spain manufactures the full barrel skin for sections of the rear fuselage; the horizontal tail plane boxes are manufactured at Puerto Real in the south of the country. At the Airbus facility in Getafe, the horizontal stabiliser section is assembled and tested together with production of the rearmost fuselage barrel.

At Broughton in North Wales, the wing framework, or wing box, is constructed from aluminium front and rear spars and aluminium-lithium ribs. Single piece carbon fibre-reinforced polymer (CFRP) upper and lower wing covers are mated to the wing framework, which, when complete, has the fuel tanks, hydraulic components, electrical and pneumatic systems and internal structures installed in the wing box. The wings are then transported to Bremen for fitting out.

The aircraft's structural sections are transported by road, sea and air from the Airbus factories to the final assembly line (FAL) in the French city of Toulouse. Airbus' fleet of

A300-600ST Beluga and A330-743L Beluga XL aircraft are used to deliver the sections by air. The FAL is an L-shaped facility covering 116,000 sq m, named after Roger Béteille, who was an aeronautical engineer at Airbus between 1967 and 1985 and regarded as the father of the company. The FAL consists of two buildings: the main aircraft assembly hall with adjacent workshops, services and stores, and a second building containing a smaller aircraft hall for indoor ground testing and cabin pre-customisation, together with a logistics hall, technical centre and offices. The FAL comprises a number of different stations numbered in descending order, where aircraft sections are progressively added to the airframe, both externally and internally, until the aircraft becomes more complete.

Assembly begins at Station 59. The forward, centre and rear fuselage sections, which already have some components pre-installed, are fitted out with cabin monuments, including the galleys, toilets and crew rest compartments. The fuselage sections then move to Station 50 where they are joined, using lasers to carefully align the sections, and further fitted out internally, including finishing off the crew rest area and rear galley. The nose landing gear is also installed at this station. On completion, the mated fuselage is transferred as a single entity on a transporter to Station 40.

At Station 40 the wings and tail assembly, including the vertical and horizontal stabilisers and the tail cone, are joined to the fuselage. The main landing gear is installed, engine pylons are fitted to the now connected wings and the first fuselage electrical power-on takes place enabling some function tests and wiring checks. Cabin furnishing also begins at Station 40, including the fitting of the floor, sidewalls, overhead storage compartments and ceiling panels.

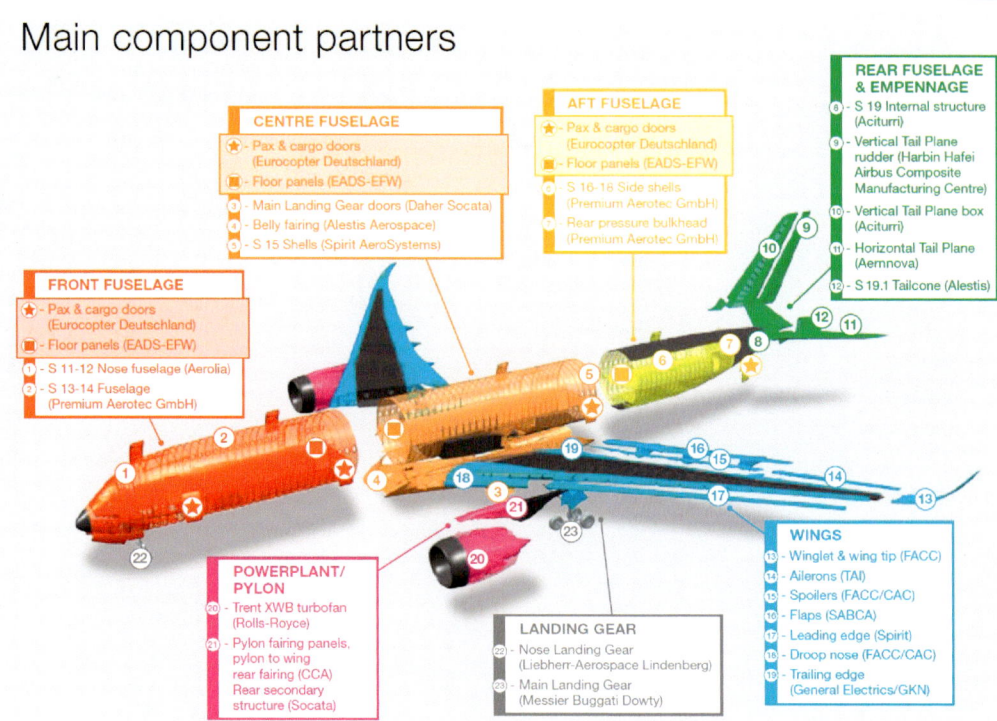

The main component partners involved in building the A350. (Airbus)

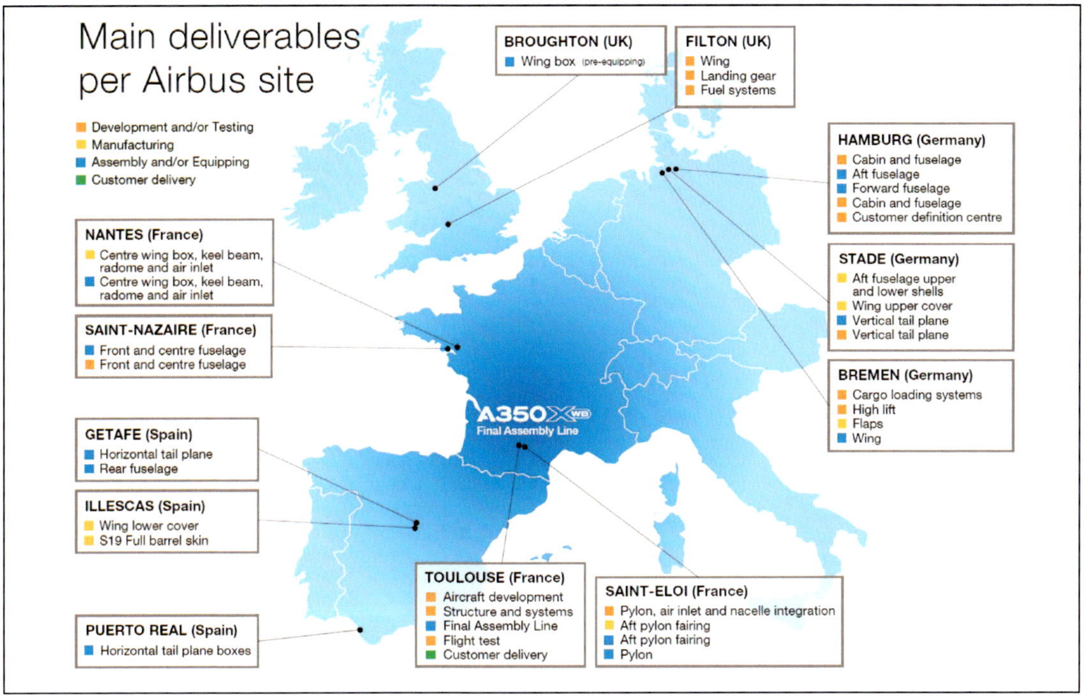

The various Airbus sites across Europe and their key responsibilities in the production of the A350. (Airbus)

The Airbus factory in Getafe, Spain, is responsible for the final production of the horizontal tail plane. (Pablo Cabellos/Airbus)

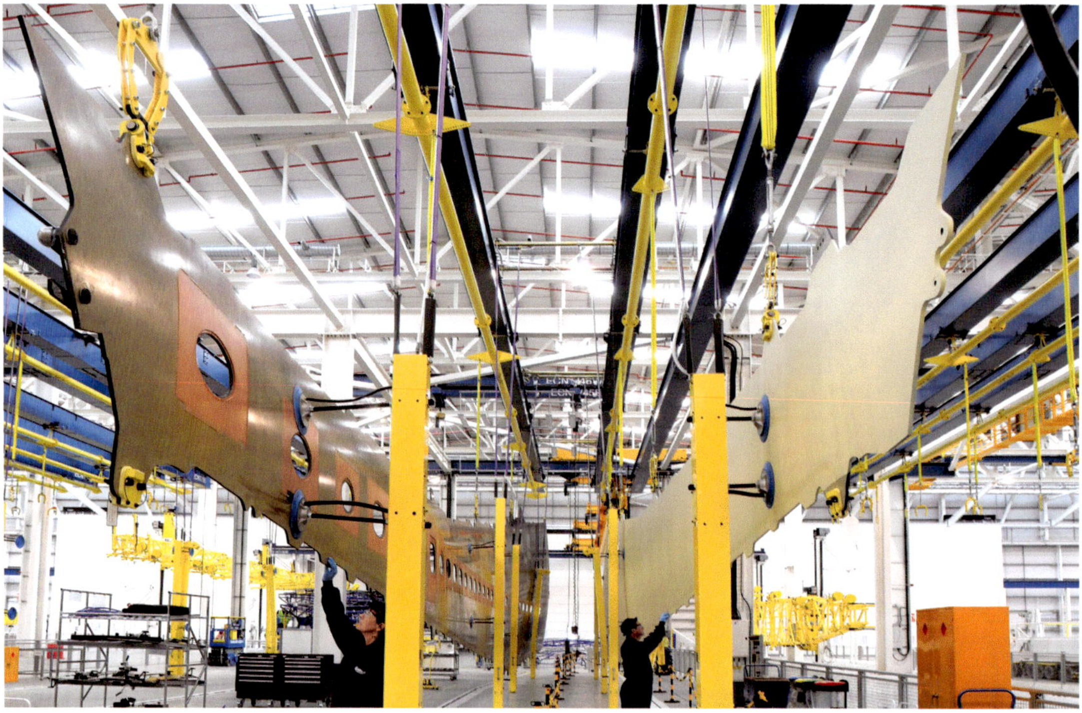

Suspended lower and upper all composite A350 wing covers in the Airbus wing factory at Broughton, Wales. (M. Chainey/Airbus)

A350 wing box section before the electrics, hydraulics and flight control surfaces are installed. (British Airways)

Above: Airbus introduced Beluga XLs in 2020 to transport major sub-assembly sections to the final assembly line at Toulouse, France. (MarcelX42, CC BY-SA 4.0)

Right: A set of A350 wings being unloaded from a Beluga XL at Toulouse. (Airbus)

Front fuselage section of an A350-1041 being moved into the main final assembly hall. (Philippe Masclet/Airbus)

Above: Centre fuselage section of an A350-941 entering the final assembly hall at Toulouse. (Alexandre Doumenjou/Airbus)

Below: Rear fuselage section of an A350-1041 at Toulouse. (Philippe Masclet/Airbus)

At this point, the aircraft is moved on its own wheels for the first time and towed to Station 30, where the installation of more exterior parts including the belly fairing and landing gear doors takes place. Additional cabin installation is completed, including seats and their cabling, partitions, galley equipment and the cargo compartment linings. The full aircraft electrical power-on test and indoor ground testing of the mechanical, electrical and avionics systems also take place at Station 30, followed by outdoor, cabin-related, ground testing at Station 18, which includes cabin pressurisation, air conditioning, in-flight entertainment system connectivity and cabin intercommunication data systems. The fuel gauges are calibrated and tested at this stage and all the passenger and cargo doors are assessed and adjusted, as required.

From Station 18 the aircraft moves to the paint shop, where paint is applied using an electrostatic spray system which increases efficiency by reducing overspray and results in the paint being applied more evenly on the aircraft. Polyurethane paints are used as they are resistant to chemicals, solvents and abrasion.

The last assembly stage takes place at Station 20, where the cabin furnishing is completed with the fitting of curtains and safety equipment, along with the in-flight entertainment system, premium seating and bespoke trim and finishes. Cockpit furnishing is also undertaken, including fitting of the cockpit seats. Externally, the

The various fuselage sections are moved into the final assembly hall before joining. (Hervé Goussé/Airbus)

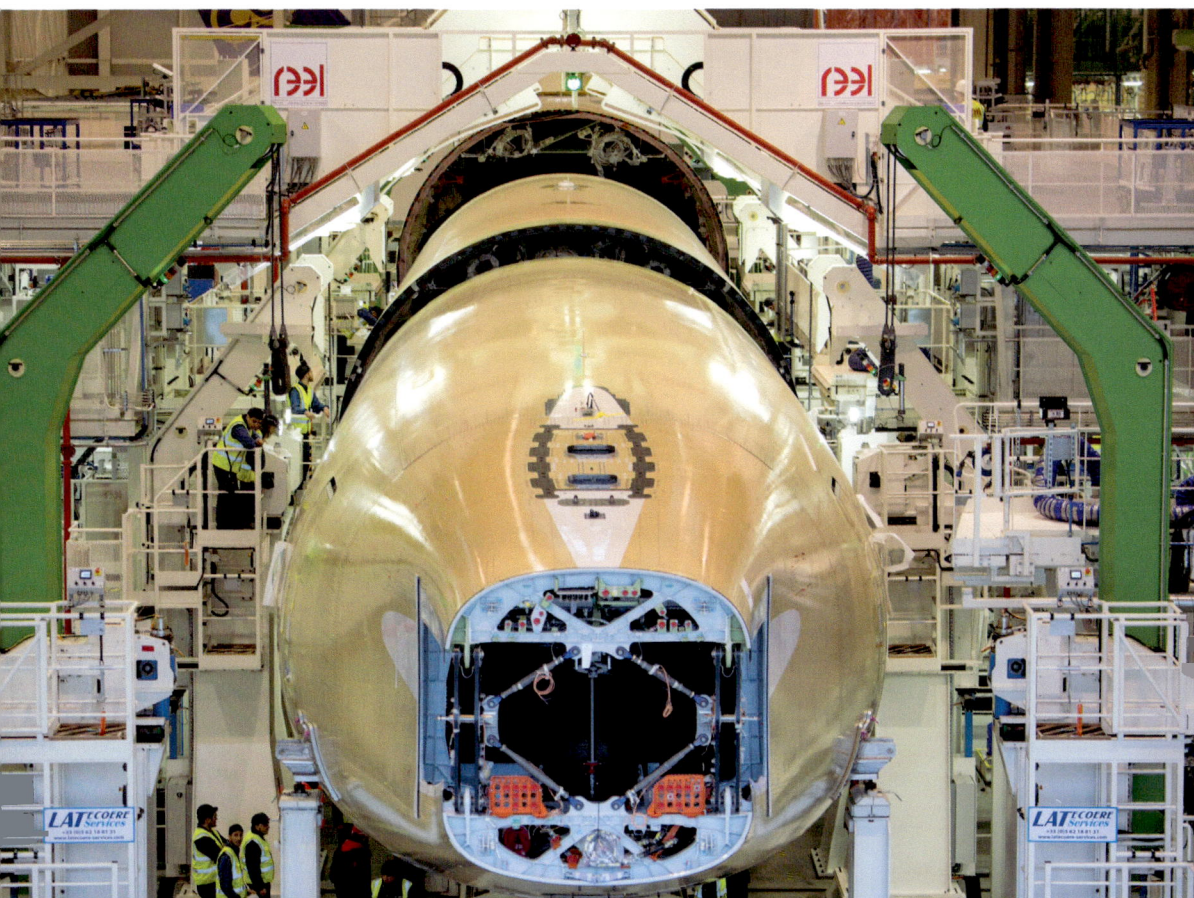

Rolls-Royce Trent XWB engines are installed at this station, along with the auxiliary power unit.

The final ground checks, conducted with the customer, are carried out at the Airbus Flight Testing and Delivery Centre and include external surfaces and paint, cabin visual inspection, static aircraft system and flight deck checks and static engine runs. These are followed by several test flights, including the customer acceptance flight, to check all the aircraft systems and handling in the entire flight envelope. On satisfactory completion of the technical checks and tests, documentation confirming the aircraft's compliance with the type certificate and technical specification is signed and the Certificate of Airworthiness for the airframe is issued. Finally, aircraft ownership is transferred to the customer and the aircraft is delivered.

At a full production rate of nine to ten aircraft per month, each A350 takes approximately two and a half months to complete from the beginning of final assembly to final delivery to the customer.

In 2020 Airbus began the completion and delivery of some A350s at its facility in Tianjin, North China. Initial assembly of the A350s is completed at Toulouse before the aircraft are flown to Tianjin where they undergo final cabin installation, painting and flight testing at the Airbus Tianjin Widebody Completion and Delivery Centre before delivery to the customer. At the end of 2024, Airbus Tianjin had delivered twenty-five A350s.

Lasers are used to carefully align the fuselage sections before they are joined together. (Frederic Lancelot/Airbus)

Fitting of the vertical tail plane (vertical stabiliser) on an A350-941, which is destined for China Airlines. (Hervé Goussé/Airbus)

Winglet fitting on a Virgin Atlantic A350-1041. (Jean-Baptiste Accariez/Airbus)

Above: Station 40 of the final assembly line where the wings and tail assembly, including the vertical and horizontal stabilisers and the tail cone, are joined to the fuselage. (Hervé Goussé/Airbus)

Below: An A350-941 rolls out of Station 40 on its own wheels for the first time. (Artem Tchaikovski/Airbus)

Above: Installation of a Rolls-Royce Trent XWB-84 engine. (Philippe Masclet/Airbus)

Below: Painting the fuselage of an Air Caraïbes A350-1041. (Pascal Pigeyre/Airbus)

Chapter 3

Airbus A350-900: Into Service

The A350-900 received approval for Extended-range Twin-engine Operations Performance Standards (ETOPS) 'beyond 180 minutes' diversion time from the European Aviation Safety Agency (EASA) in October 2014, prior to entry into service. This was the first time a new aircraft type had received this level of ETOPS before starting commercial services. The approval also included the option for ETOPS300 and ETOPS370, depending on individual operator selection. ETOPS370 extended the maximum diversion time to 370 minutes at a one-engine inoperative cruise speed, equivalent to a maximum diversion distance of 2,500 nm.

Airbus delivered the first production A350-900 to launch customer Qatar Airways during a ceremony at Toulouse on 22 December 2014. Registered as A7-ALA, the aircraft was initially used for crew training and familiarisation during short-haul flights in the Middle East. The first revenue flight took place on 15 January 2015 from Doha to Frankfurt. By the end of 2015, Qatar Airways had a fleet of eight A350-900s from an initial order for thirty-four of the variant.

Vietnam Airlines was the second airline to operate the A350-900 following delivery of its first aircraft, on lease from AerCap, at the end of June 2015. The A350 was initially introduced into commercial service on domestic routes between Hanoi and Ho Chi Minh City. Long-haul routes were subsequently added, beginning with services from Hanoi and Ho Chi Minh City to Paris. Carrying either 305 or 323 passengers, depending on the operation, in a three-class seating configuration, the A350s operate all over the Asia-Pacific region, serving cities such as Seoul, Busan, Osaka and Nagoya, and the major Australian cities of Melbourne and Sydney. They are also deployed on routes to European and some North American destinations.

Finnair was the first airline in Europe (third in the world) to begin operating the A350-900, placing an initial order for eleven aircraft plus eight options in 2007 with conversion of the options to firm orders in December 2014. The first of Finnair's new A350 aircraft (OH-LWA) arrived in Helsinki in October 2015, with two more delivered by the end of the year. Finnair initially used its A350s on intra-European routes from Helsinki, beginning with Amsterdam. By the end of November 2015 the aircraft had been introduced onto long-haul routes, including Bangkok, Beijing, Hong Kong and Singapore, and to the

US by the end of the year. Finnair currently has eighteen A350-900s in its fleet, operating them in a three-class seating configuration.

On 2 May 2016 the Federal Aviation Administration (FAA) approved the A350-900 for ETOPS beyond 180 minutes diversion time, including provisions for ETOPS300 (corresponding to a maximum diversion distance of 2,000 nm), which would allow for more direct and efficient routings across the North and Mid-Pacific from the USA to South-East Asia and Australasia.

The timing of the FAA's approval was particularly favourable for Delta Air Lines, the first airline from North America to take delivery of the A350-900. The carrier received the first of the twenty-five A350s it had initially ordered, in July 2017. Configured with 306 seats, the A350s were purchased to allow Delta to phase out its Boeing 747-400s and primarily operated routes from its Detroit hub to Asia, starting with Tokyo-Narita, Seoul and Beijing. Once the A350-900 had accumulated additional in-service hours, it was granted a further provision for ETOPS370 by the FAA.

In January 2025 the A350-900 marked its tenth anniversary in commercial service. As of 31 July 2025 there have been 1,009 firm orders for the A350-900, 571 of which have been delivered. The A350-900 is currently operated by thirty-five airlines. Seven carriers have A350-900s on order but still await the delivery of their first examples, including Aircalin (two), Egyptair, Indigo, Kuwait Airways and United Airlines. Afriqiyah Airways has ten A350-900s on order and Libyan Airlines is expecting six of the type. However, years of civil war in Libya have made it likely that these orders will be either renegotiated and swapped to other Airbus types or cancelled.

Qatar Airways was the launch customer of the A350-900 and received its first aircraft, A7-ALA, shown here, on 22 December 2014. (Gerard van der Schaaf, CC BY 2.0)

Above: The second airline to operate the A350-941 was Vietnam Airlines, taking delivery of its first aircraft (VN-A886) in June 2015. (Steven Byles, CC BY-SA 2.0)

Left: Delta Air Lines, the first airline from North America to take delivery of the A350-941, received its first A350 (N501DN, shown here) in July 2017. (Alan Wilson, CC BY-SA 2.0)

Below: Finnair was the first airline in Europe to operate the A350-941, taking delivery of its first aircraft (OH-LWA) in early October 2015. (Valentin Hintikka, CC BY 2.0)

Operators

Europe

There are currently twelve carriers in Europe operating the A350-900. Air France has a fleet of thirty-nine from an initial order for forty-one A350s, and received its first aircraft in September 2019. The Air France-KLM Group ordered an additional fifty A350s (combined A350-900 and A350-1000 order), plus purchase rights for forty more, in September 2023, with deliveries due to begin in 2026. The variant breakdown is yet to be disclosed. Air France is investing in the A350 for fleet renewal and sustainability reasons, as the carrier looks to replace its aging Airbus A330s and Boeing 777s.

Spanish flag carrier Iberia has a fleet of twenty-three A350-900s. Its initial aircraft, received in June 2018, was the first A350 to feature a performance improvement package, including aerodynamic changes such as higher, extended winglets together with structural improvements leading to an increased maximum take-off weight capability. Similarly, Iberia was the first airline to receive an A350 with the new production standard 2022, which included improvements in operational performance, achieved through new flap positions, faster retraction of the landing gear and a reduction in the empty weight of the aircraft. The aircraft, which was the 500th to be delivered, offered an optimised travel experience for the passengers, through features such as a 4-in widening of the cabin at armrest level, the addition of folding and adjustable headrests, a new-generation in-flight entertainment system and a personal electronic device holder for viewing and charging devices.

Several other Spanish airlines have small fleets of A350-900s. Charter airline Iberojet has two examples (previously operated under Evelop Airlines name), which are operated in a high-density configuration, for up to 432 passengers, on short- and long-haul flights out of Spain and Portugal. World2Fly also utilises a high-density seating layout in its three A350-900s, which are used for long-haul flights out of Madrid to destinations in the Caribbean, United States and Mexico.

Along with Finnair from Scandinavia, SAS Scandinavian Airlines also operates the A350-900, with a current fleet of four aircraft. SAS took delivery of its first A350 in November 2019 and, by June 2021, had added five more aircraft. However, after filing for bankruptcy protection in July 2022, SAS halved its A350 fleet to three aircraft by ending some leasing arrangements early. One of the aircraft released in 2022 returned to the carrier in late February 2024 on an improved leasing arrangement. SAS operates its A350s in a three-class configuration, carrying up to 300 passengers on long-haul flights from Copenhagen to destinations such as New York JFK, Boston, Shanghai and Tokyo.

Lufthansa is due to become one of the largest operators of the A350-900. After receiving its first example in November 2016, it currently has a fleet of thirty-one aircraft, four of which are pre-owned examples previously operated by Philippine Airlines. Having placed orders for up to thirty additional new A350s between 2019 and 2023, the carrier is aiming to withdraw its older Boeing 747-400s and Airbus A340-300s and -600s. It has also secured six A350-900s previously operated by LATAM (four) and South African Airways (two). Lufthansa uses several three-class seating configurations accommodating between 293 and 318 passengers and, in May 2024, introduced its new Allegris cabin interior for up to 267 passengers, featuring a single row of four First Class suites in a 1-1-1-1 arrangement.

Italy's national carrier ITA Airways has a fleet of six A350-900s, all of which were acquired in 2022 as part of a fleet modernisation strategy. ITA's A350 cabins have a two-class configuration for up to 334 passengers. The type is used on ITA's intercontinental routes, including Rome to Los Angeles, San Francisco, Buenos Aries and Tokyo.

Air Caraïbes was the first French airline to introduce the A350-900 into service in 2017. It now operates three aircraft, carrying up to 389 passengers between Paris and destinations such as Pointe-à-Pitre, Fort-de-France, Cayenne, Saint Domingo and Cancun. The low-cost carrier French Bee has four aircraft in which the majority of its 411 seats are configured in a high-density layout for flights from Paris Orly Airport to destinations in the US and French Polynesia.

In March 2025 Edelweiss Air became the first Swiss airline to take delivery of an A350-900, one of six the carrier plans to acquire as part of its fleet modernisation. The aircraft, which had previously been operated by LATAM Linhas Aéreas of Brazil, was introduced into commercial service on 1 April 2025 between Zurich and Tenerife.

North and South America

Delta Air Lines is currently the only operator of the A350-900 in the US, with a fleet of thirty-eight aircraft and an additional six on order. The A350 is mainly used on the carrier's international routes out of Atlanta Hartsfield-Jackson International Airport to Europe, South America, South Africa and Asia. It also features on some high-capacity domestic routes from Atlanta, including Las Vegas, Los Angeles and Detroit.

United Airlines placed an initial order for twenty-five A350-900s in 2010. The order altered to thirty-five A350-1000s in 2013 and finally to forty-five A350-900s in 2017. The delivery date was also deferred from 2020 to 2027 and, more recently, to 2030. It has been suggested that United will eventually use the A350s to replace its Boeing-777ER fleet, which is still relatively young.

There are currently no operators of the A350-900 in South America. LATAM Linhas Aéreas of Brazil acquired thirteen A350s between May 2016 and January 2021. At least five aircraft, delivered in July 2020 and January 2021, were stored and never entered into service with LATAM due to the Covid-19 pandemic. The carrier filed for Chapter 11

Airbus A350-941 F-HTYF of Air France. (Steven He)

bankruptcy in May 2020 due to the impact of the pandemic on the aviation industry. The A350s were returned to respective lessors as part of the airline's recovery plans.

Azul Linhas Aéreas Brasileiras operated two A350s for less than a year during 2023. The aircraft were acquired in September and December 2022 as part of the carrier's fleet renewal plan to replace its Airbus A330-200s. After several months of crew and maintenance training, the A350s entered into service, flying from Campinas to destinations such as Paris, Lisbon and Orlando. However, Azul ceased A350 operations in late October 2023. The precise reasons for their withdrawal were not disclosed, although reports suggest that the airline considered the A350 to have high maintenance and operational costs, despite its fuel burn efficiencies, and favoured the new A330-900neo.

Above: Airbus A350-941 F-HTYQ, shown here at Boston Logan International Airport, USA, was delivered to Air France in May 2022. (4300streetcar, CC BY 4.0)

Below: Spanish flag carrier Iberia has a fleet of twenty-three A350-941s, including EC-NBE, which was delivered in January 2019. (Iberia)

Airbus A350-941 EC-MYX *Paco de Lucia* of Iberia. (Iberia)

Economy cabin of Iberia's A350-941 with a 3-3-3 seating configuration. (Iberia)

Spanish-Portuguese charter airline Evelop Airlines acquired two A350-941s in March 2019 and 2020, including EC-NBO pictured here, before the carrier was renamed Iberojet in 2021. (Bene Riobó, CC BY-SA 4.0)

Airbus A350-941 EC-NGY of Iberojet, one of two A350s acquired from Evelop Airlines in 2021. (Bahnfrend, CC BY-SA 4.0)

Top: Spanish carrier World2Fly currently has a fleet of three A350-941s, including EC-NOI. (Anna Zvereva, CC BY-SA 2.0)

Above: Finnair A350-941 OH-LWL painted in 'Marimekko Kivet' special livery. (Anna Zvereva, CC BY-SA 2.0)

Left: Business Class cabin in Finnair's A350-941s. (Finnair)

SAS Scandinavian Airlines operates a fleet of four A350-941s including SE-RSE, which was delivered in March 2021. (N509FZ, CC BY-SA 4.0)

Germany's flag carrier Lufthansa is one of the largest operators of the A350-941. D-AIXG is pictured during take-off at Munich Airport. (Juke Schweizer, CC BY-SA 4.0)

Lufthansa A350-941 D-AIXP painted in the revised Lufthansa livery, which was introduced in 2018. (MarcelX42, CC BY-SA 4.0)

Italian national airline ITA Airways acquired its six A350-941s in 2022 including EI-IFE. (Mark Bess, CC BY-SA 2.0)

Airbus A350-941 EI-IFF of ITA Airways departing from Tokyo Haneda International Airport, Japan. (Steven Byles, CC BY-SA 2.0)

Air Caraïbes A350-941 F-HNET on final approach to Paris Orly Airport. (Olivier Cabaret, CC BY 2.0)

Low-cost carrier French Bee has a fleet of four A350-941s. F-HREU was the first example to be acquired by the airline in January 2018. (Dylan Agbagni)

Edelweiss Air became the first Swiss airline to operate the Airbus A350-941 when it took delivery of its first example (HB-IHF) in March 2025. (Edelweiss Air)

Above: Delta Air Lines are currently the only operator of the A350-941 in the USA with a fleet of thirty-eight aircraft, including N508DN pictured here. (Alan Wilson, CC BY-SA 2.0)

Below: LATAM Linhas Aéreas of Brazil acquired thirteen A350-941s between May 2016 and January 2021, including PR-XTC pictured here. Due to financial problems all aircraft had been returned to respective lessors by August 2021. (Rafael Luiz Canossa, CC BY-SA 2.0)

Airbus A350-941 PR-AOY of Azul Linhas Aéreas Brasileiras, one of two A350-941s operated by the carrier in 2023. (Semduvidas1, CC BY-SA 4.0)

West and Central Asia

Turkish Airlines has continued to grow its fleet of A350-900s since taking delivery of its first example in October 2020. The airline currently operates a fleet of twenty-nine aircraft and placed orders for a further sixty-four as part of its fleet modernisation and sustainable expansion strategy in 2023. The A350s operate a mixture of regional and long-haul flights.

Russian state carrier Aeroflot has seven A350-900s from an order for twenty-two aircraft. However, deliveries ceased after the invasion of Ukraine by Russian forces in 2022. Sanctions also prevent the export of spare parts from the EU and USA to Russia, which has had severe consequences for the operation of these aircraft on domestic routes. In late 2024 it was reported that, after a brief period in storage, six of Aeroflot's seven A350s were active and operating under Russian registrations.

East and Southern Asia

Air China is the largest operator and the first airline to take ownership of the A350-900 in mainland China. The airline received its first example in August 2018 and gradually built up a fleet of thirty aircraft by December 2023. The A350 is used on both domestic and long-haul international routes.

China Eastern Airlines and China Southern Airlines each have fleets of twenty A350-900s, which were first introduced into service in 2019. Sichuan Airlines, the largest carrier in Western China, received its first A350-900 in August 2018, as an additional Airbus type in its all-Airbus fleet. The airline operates a fleet of nine A350-900s, with five still on order.

Taiwan's China Airlines operates fifteen A350-900s on its European, North American, and Australasian network. The A350s are configured in a three-class seating layout and carry up to 306 passengers. Fellow Taiwanese carrier Starlux Airlines took delivery of its first A350-900, from an initial order for eighteen aircraft, in October 2022. An additional five examples were ordered in March 2019. The airline currently has ten aircraft in its fleet, which it operates in a four-class configuration carrying 306 passengers, including four First Class suites, from its Taipei hub to destinations such as Bangkok, Tokyo, Los Angeles and San Francisco.

Hainan Airlines operated nine A350-900s between September 2018 and March 2024. It withdrew four aircraft from October 2019 and February 2020, with the other examples either sold or returned to the lessor between September 2022 and March 2024. The decision to end the use of the A350 was taken by the carrier's holding company, Fangda Aviation, after undergoing restructuring due to financial issues and the impact of the Covid-19 pandemic. Fangda Aviation is also the parent holding company of Hong Kong Airlines, which acquired six A350-900s between August 2017 and November 2018, before beginning to withdraw them from service from August 2019 through to February 2020.

Cathay Pacific Airways, the flag carrier of Hong Kong, has a fleet of thirty A350-900s, which it operates on both short-medium-haul regional and long-haul routes. It took delivery of its first example in May 2016; the thirtieth and final aircraft from its initial order arriving in late December 2023.

Japan Airlines (JAL) placed an initial order for eighteen A350-900s in October 2013 and received its first example in June 2019. This aircraft was designated for use on busy domestic routes, featuring 369 seats and a lower maximum take-off weight. The carrier currently has a fleet of sixteen. JAL lost one of its A350-900s (JA13XJ) on 2 January 2024 after a ground collision with a Japanese Coast Guard De Havilland Canada Dash 8 at Tokyo's Haneda Airport shortly after the A350 had touched down. In March 2024 JAL ordered an additional twenty-one A350-900s, of which twenty were to be used on international routes alongside its fleet of A350-1000s, and one was configured for domestic routes to replace the aircraft lost in January 2024.

Singapore Airlines is currently the world's largest operator of the A350-900. The carrier took delivery of its first A350 in March 2016 and has since built a fleet of sixty-five aircraft. Singapore initially acquired the A350-900 to replace some of its Boeing 777-300ERs on European routes. In October 2018 it became the first airline to introduce the A350-900ULR (ultra long range) variant into service, proceeding to operate seven of the type on non-stop flights between Singapore and US cities, including Newark Liberty, New York and San Francisco. Later in the same year Singapore Airlines began to operate a lower weight variant of the A350-900, powered by lower thrust XWB-75 engines which were originally developed for the A350-800. Referred to as the A350 Medium Haul, it is the highest capacity version of the A350s used by the airline, having 303 seats, and mainly operates regional flights.

Twenty Airbus A350-900s were part of a substantial order for 470 aircraft placed by Air India in February 2023. The carrier received its first example in December 2023 and, by May 2024, had acquired five more aircraft. Air India initially used the A350s on domestic services, before employing them on international flights from Delhi to Dubai at the beginning of May 2024.

The A350-900 became the flagship of South Korean carrier Asiana Airlines' long-distance routes when it was introduced into service in 2017. The airline has a fleet of fifteen A350s, which it operates on regional routes to north and south-east Asia and on long-haul routes to destinations in North America, Australia and Europe. Another South Korean airline, Korean Air, signed a contract with Airbus in March 2024 to acquire six A350-900s. It received its first two examples in December 2024.

The flag carrier of Thailand, Thai Airways, has a fleet of twenty-three A350-900s and received its first example in August 2016. Following delivery of the initial twelve aircraft by May 2018, there was a hiatus of five years before Thai Airways secured a deal to lease eleven more A350s, which were delivered over a twelve-month period from May 2023. Thai deploys its A350s on short-, medium- and long-haul routes.

Turkish Airlines is destined to become one of the largest operators of the A350. It currently operates twenty-nine examples out of an order for ninety aircraft. Pictured here is A350-941 TC-LGH, which was delivered in February 2023. (Mitchul Hope, CC BY-SA 2.0)

Turkish Airlines took delivery of Airbus A350-941 TC-LGD in March 2021. (Md Shaifuzzaman Ayon, CC BY-SA 4.0)

49

Vietnam Airlines was the first Asian airline to take delivery of the A350-900. It has a fleet of fourteen aircraft operating to destinations in Vietnam, north-east Asia, Australia, Europe and North America.

Other operators of the A350-900 include Philippine Airlines, which operates two A350-900s on long-haul intercontinental routes from its Manila hub, and Malaysia Airlines, which has seven A350-900s in its fleet, of which almost all were delivered between November 2017 and July 2018, the latest arriving in November 2023.

Russian state carrier Aeroflot has a fleet of seven A350-941s, including VQ-BFY, the first example to be delivered to the airline in February 2020. (Colin Cooke, CC BY-SA 2.0)

Air China A350-941 B-1086 taxiing in at Beijing Capital International Airport, China. (Alan Wilson, CC BY-SA 2.0)

Air China has a fleet of thirty A350-941s. Pictured here is A350 B-1083, which was painted in 'Expo 2019 Beijing' special colours until November 2019. (Alan Wilson, CC BY-SA 2.0)

China Eastern Airlines introduced the A350-941 into service in early 2019. The example shown here is B-323H, the first A350 to be completed at Airbus' Tianjin plant in North China. (N509FZ, CC BY-SA 4.0)

Airbus A350-941 B-305X of China Eastern Airlines. (Windmemories, CC BY-SA 4.0)

China Southern Airlines A350-941 B-309W at Beijing Capital International Airport, China. (N509FZ, CC BY-SA 4.0)

Airbus A350-941 B-30EA was delivered to China Southern Airlines in November 2020. (Md Shaifuzzaman Ayon, CC BY-SA 4.0)

Sichuan Airlines A350-941 B-325J painted in 'Panda Route' special colour scheme. (N509FZ, CC BY-SA 4.0)

Sichuan Airlines currently operates a fleet of nine A350-900s, including A350-941 B-304V. (N509FZ, CC BY-SA 4.0)

China Airlines A350-941 B-18918 on final approach to London Heathrow Airport. (Richard Blata)

Airbus A350-941 B-18901 of China Airlines painted in 'Mikado Pheasant/Syrmaticus Mikado' special colour scheme. (ltdccba, CC BY-SA 2.0)

Taiwanese carrier Starlux Airlines currently has ten A350-941s in its fleet, including B-58504. (Simply Aviation, CC BY 4.0)

Taiwanese carrier Starlux Airlines took delivery of Airbus A350-941 B-58501 in October 2022. (Steven Byles, CC BY-SA 2.0)

Airbus A350-941 B-1070 of Hainan Airlines landing at Beijing Capital International Airport, China. (N509FZ, CC BY-SA 4.0)

Hong Kong Airlines operated up to six A350-941s between August 2017 and February 2020 before withdrawing the type due to financial issues. A350-941 B-LGD, pictured here, was delivered in February 2018. (N509FZ, CC BY-SA 4.0)

Airbus A350-941 B-LQD of Cathay Pacific Airways, one of the largest operators of the A350. (Author's collection)

Cathay Pacific's Airbus A350-941 B-LRP taxiing out at Manchester Airport. (Author's collection)

Japan Airlines A350-941 JA04XJ was painted in a '20th Arashi Thanks Jet' special colour scheme between November 2019 and January 2021. (Melv_L-MACASR, CC BY-SA 2.0)

Airbus A350-941 JA04XJ of Japan Airlines at Tokyo International Airport, Japan, in August 2023. (SuFlyer)

Singapore Airlines acquired its first A350-941 in March 2016 and has subsequently built a fleet of sixty-five aircraft. Taxiing at Manchester Airport is 9V-SMF, Airbus's 10,000th aircraft. (Author's collection)

Singapore Airlines A350-941 9V-SMA being prepared for its next flight, showing the forward and aft cargo compartment doors and the four passenger cabin doors on the right-hand side of the A350-941. The door for the bulk cargo compartment is on the left-hand side of the aircraft. (Aero Pixels, CC BY 2.0)

Air India's first A350-941, VT-JRA, which was delivered in December 2023. (Air India)

South Korean flagship carrier Asiana Airlines currently has a fleet of fifteen A350-941s including HL8360, pictured here at Frankfurt Airport, Germany. (MarcelX42, CC BY-SA 4.0)

Airbus A350-941 HL8362 of Asiana Airlines at Los Angeles International Airport, USA, in November 2021. (Charles, CC BY 2.0)

Korean Air received its first two A350s in late December 2024, including A350-941HL8598. (Lars Rohde)

Airbus A350-941 HS-THG of Thai Airways about to land at Melbourne International Airport, Australia. (Mitchul Hope, CC BY-SA 2.0)

Thai Airways has a fleet of twenty-three A350-900s, including A350-941 HS-THN. (Md Shaifuzzaman Ayon, CC BY-SA 4.0)

Vietnam Airlines A350-941 VN-A887 taxiing after arrival at Narita International Airport, Tokyo, Japan. (Alan Wilson, CC BY-SA 2.0)

Airbus A350-941 9M-MAF is one of seven A350-941s operated by Malaysian Airlines. (John Taggart, CC BY-SA 2.0)

Philippine Airlines currently has two A350-941s in its fleet including RP-C3508, named *The Love Bus*. (Mark Bess, CC BY-SA 2.0)

Africa

Two airlines from Africa currently operate the A350-900: Ethiopian Airlines and Air Mauritius. Ethiopian Airlines has a fleet of twenty A350-900s, which have 348 seats configured in a two-class layout. The carrier flies the A350 from its Addis Ababa hub to destinations within Africa, Asia, Europe, the Middle East and North America. In November 2023, Ethiopian signed a Memorandum of Understanding for eleven additional A350-900s.

Air Mauritius received its first two A350-900s from Airbus in October and November 2017. It increased its fleet to four in 2020 with the acquisition of two former South African Airways A350s. At the Paris Airshow in 2023, the carrier confirmed an order for an additional three aircraft to strengthen its current route provision and to secure expansion of its European and south-east Asia networks.

South African Airlines leased four A350-900s in November 2019, but their use was short-lived and they were suddenly returned to their respective lessors in March–April 2020 due to financial difficulties and future uncertainty associated with the early months of the COVID-19 pandemic.

Middle East

Qatar Airways is currently the largest operator of the A350-900 having thirty-four aircraft. The carrier also sub-leased four examples from LATAM Linhas Aéreas in March/April 2017 due to delays in the delivery of its ordered aircraft. Of these, two were returned towards the end of the year and the other two were retained until March 2020. LATAM was again the supplier of an additional three A350s sub-leased by Qatar Airways from 2019 to March 2020, at which stage Qatar was looking to reduce its fleet due to the advent of the COVID-19 pandemic. From January 2021 to January 2023 at least twenty-three of Qatar's A350-900s were grounded for between nine and twenty-seven months due to surface paint degradation concerns and subsequent legal action; new aircraft deliveries were not accepted until the problem was resolved. Qatar Airways and Airbus reached an agreeable settlement to the legal dispute in February 2023. Qatar's current A350s have a two-class seating layout for 283 passengers.

The world's largest international airline Emirates has ordered sixty-five A350-900s. The carrier took delivery of its first A350 on 25 November 2024 and eight more have subsequently been accepted. Emirates' first A350 entered into commercial service on 3 January 2025, operating an inaugural flight from Dubai to Edinburgh. In July 2025 Emirates was using the A350 on services to thirteen destinations, including Edinburgh, Mumbai, Ahmedabad, Kuwait, Bahrain, Amman, Bologna, Colombo, Dammam, Istabul, Lyon, Muscat and Tunis, with more global destinations to be introduced in the coming months.

Meanwhile, Kuwait Airways is still awaiting delivery of its first order of two A350-900s. The carrier originally ordered ten A350s in 2014 but subsequently swapped some orders for Airbus A330neos and reduced the order to two aircraft in August 2023.

In November 2023 Egyptair placed an order for ten A350-900s; deliveries are expected to begin in 2025 through to 2027.

Australasia

Fiji Airways is currently the only operator of the A350-900 in Australasia. The carrier took delivery of its first two examples in November/December 2019. An additional two aircraft were acquired in August 2023. The A350s are configured in a two-class layout with 334 seats. They are used on services between Fiji and Australia and New Zealand, as well as on long-haul routes to Hong Kong, San Francisco and Vancouver; the latest aircraft providing opportunities for the carrier to increase capacity on its popular routes and expand its long-haul network.

Ethiopian Airlines' A350-941 ET-ATQ at London Heathrow Airport. (John Taggart, CC BY-SA 2.0)

Airbus A350-941 ET-AYB of Ethiopian Airlines on short-final to London Heathrow Airport. (Mike Burdett, CC BY-SA 2.0)

Airbus A350-941 3B-NBQ of Air Mauritius landing at Paris Charles de Gaulle Airport, France. (Olivier Cabaret, CC BY 2.0)

South African Airlines leased four A350-941s in November 2019, including ZS-SDF shown here at New York JFK Airport. However, they were returned to their respective lessors in March–April 2020 due to financial issues. (Adam Moreira, CC BY-SA 4.0)

Qatar Airways is currently the leading Middle Eastern operator of the A350-941 with thirty-four aircraft. A7-ALO, pictured here at Manchester Airport, was delivered in October 2017. (Author's collection)

Airbus A350-941 A7-ALZ of Qatar Airways painted in 'oneworld' special livery. (Md Shaifuzzaman Ayon, CC BY-SA 4.0)

Emirates' first A350-941, A6-EXA, entered commercial service on 3 January 2023, operating its inaugural flight from Dubai International Airport to Edinburgh, Scotland. (Emirates)

Emirates A350-941 A6-EXA arriving at Edinburgh Airport, Scotland, following its first scheduled service. (Emirates)

Fiji Airways' A350-941 DQ-FAJ at Sydney Airport, Australia. This aircraft was delivered to Fiji Airways in December 2019. (Windmemories, CC BY-SA 4.0)

Chapter 4

Airbus A350-1000

Airbus developed the A350-1000 to replace its four-engine A340-600 and to compete with the Boeing 777-300ER and 777-9. The A350-1000 is 22 ft 11 in (6.99 m) longer than the A350-900, the extra length being achieved by the introduction of five additional fuselage frames in front of the wing (between doors 1 and 2) and six more behind the wing (between doors 3 and 4). The fuselage is identical in diameter to the A350-900. The increase in length means that the A350-1000 can accommodate an additional fifty-four passengers in a typical two-class seating configuration. Although the wingspan of the A350-1000 is the same as the -900, it has a 4 per cent (22.3 sq m; 240 sq ft) larger wing area due to a trailing edge extension, which extends the high-lift devices and the ailerons generating greater lift and lower take-off and landing speeds. The A350-1000 is equipped with the more powerful Rolls-Royce Trent XWB-97 engines, six-wheel main land gear bogies and a strengthened nose landing gear to handle the increased maximum take-off weight of 710,000 lb (322.0 tonnes).

Airbus started to assemble the first major fuselage components of the A350-1000 in September 2015 at both Hamburg and Saint-Nazaire. The forward fuselage section was delivered to Hamburg by Premium Aerotec, a subsidiary of Airbus, where it was equipped before being flown to Saint-Nazaire for mating with the pre-assembled and equipped nose fuselage section. Assembly of the first A350-1000 wings had commenced at Broughton, North Wales, a month earlier.

The final assembly of the first A350-1000 (F-WMIL; MSN059) began at Toulouse in February 2016. The prototype emerged from the paint shop at the beginning of August. It was fitted with a full suite of flight test instrumentation and, after three months of ground testing, completed its first flight on 24 November 2016. The flight over south-west France lasted 4 hours and 18 minutes, during which the crew completed initial handling trials at 10,000 ft before climbing to 25,000 ft for further systems tests and exploration of the flight envelope in both direct and normal control law.

Prior to the maiden flight the Trent XWB-97 engine was tested on the Airbus A380 engine testbed during two test campaigns of 148 and 157 flight hours respectively between November 2015 and December 2016. This followed an extensive period of ground testing, which involved eight development engines and included a 150-hour endurance test, with more than 16 hours at maximum take-off thrust and over 42 hours at maximum continuous thrust. The Trent XWB-97 received formal flight certification from EASA on 31 August 2017.

Two additional A350-1000s joined the flight test and certification programme. MSN071 (F-WWXL) made its maiden flight on 10 January 2017 and MSN065 (F-WLXV) on 7 February 2017. The test and certification responsibilities of each aircraft included:

MSN059/F-WMIL	Aerodynamic performance testing, including expansion of the flight envelope, trials of handing qualities, systems testing, engine trials, altitude testing at Toluca, Mexico, La Paz, Bolivia and Cayenne, French Guiana, and cold weather testing at Iqaluit, Canada.
MSN071/F-WWXL	Fitted with flight test instrumentation and responsible for performance evaluation, including high altitude and hot and humid weather trials in Bolivia and Colombia and extreme cold weather trials (air temperatures between -28 degrees and -37 degrees Centigrade) at Iqaluit, Canada, braking tests, and additional engine, systems and autopilot testing to supplement the work undertaken by the first test aircraft.
MSN065/F-WLXV	A light test instrumentation fit and equipped with a fully functional cabin to evaluate cabin and air systems. Used for hot weather trials (temperatures in excess of 40 degrees Centigrade) at Al Ain International Airport in the United Arab Emirates, external noise testing, route proving, early long-range flights and extended-range twin-engine operations (ETOPS) approval.

The flight test and certification programme lasted just over 1,600 flight test hours; 150 of those hours involved functional and reliability testing, which took test aircraft F-WLXV across Europe and to South America and was completed in an airline-like operational environment to demonstrate the aircraft's readiness for entry into service. The full test programme, completed in less than a year, took 1,000 hours less than that for the A350-900 due to the high level of commonality of both variants and the experience and maturity gained from the A350-900 test campaign and its subsequent entry into service. The A350-1000 received type certification from both EASA and the FAA on 21 November 2017.

In late January 2018, the third test aircraft (F-WLXV) began a demonstration tour to the Middle East and Asia-Pacific region, visiting twelve destinations including Doha, Muscat, Hong Kong, Seoul, Taipei, Hanoi, Singapore, Bangkok, Sydney, Auckland, Tokyo and Manila. The purpose of the tour was to provide existing and potential airline customers, VIPs, industry influencers and the media with an opportunity to view the aircraft's exclusive features. While in Singapore the aircraft was on static display for several days at the Singapore Airshow. The tour, during which the aircraft flew almost 34,500 nm (64,000 km), demonstrated its capability to fly long-haul routes and contributed towards ETOPS validation. ETOPS 180-minute certification was obtained on 19 June 2018 and ETOPS beyond 180 minutes at the beginning of the following month.

The initial production A350-1000 (MSN088) made its first flight on 7 December 2017 and was delivered to launch customer Qatar Airways, registered as A7-ANA, on 20 February 2018. The aircraft was the first of an initial order of thirty-seven A350-1000s and the first ever Airbus aircraft to be fitted with Qsuite seats, offering the first ever double bed in Business Class. On 24 February 2018, A7-ANA completed the first commercial flight of an A350-1000 between Doha and London Heathrow.

Rolls-Royce Trent XWB-97 engine mounted on the inner port-side pylon of the Airbus A380 engine test bed. (Alexandre Doumenjou/Airbus)

First flight of the A350-1000 (F-WMIL) on 24 November 2016. (J. V. Reymondon/Airbus)

Above: The first A350-1000 during its maiden flight. (Sylvain Ramadier/Airbus)

Right: The second A350-1000 (F-WWXL) joined the test fleet in January 2017. (Alexis Boidron)

Below: A350-1000 F-WWXL during ground and flights trials in extreme cold weather conditions at Iqaluit, Canada. (Sylvain Ramadier/Airbus)

Above: A350-1000 F-WMIL coming in to land during extreme cold weather trials at Iqaluit, Canada. (Sylvain Ramadier/Airbus)

Below: High-altitude testing at La Paz, Bolivia, involving A350-1000 F-WMIL. (Sylvain Ramadier/Airbus)

Above: The third test A350-1000 aircraft, F-WLXV, conducting water trough/flooded runway tests at Istres Air Base, France. (Sylvain Ramadier/Airbus)

Below: A350-1000 F-WLXV begins an early long-range flight which traced a 12-hour flightpath around Europe, enabling passengers to evaluate the aircraft's cabin systems in realistic conditions. (Hervé Goussé/Airbus)

Operators

When the A350-1000 first took to the skies in November 2016, Airbus had already received orders for 195 aircraft from eleven customers, including Qatar Airways (thirty-seven), United Airlines (thirty-five), Cathay Pacific (twenty-six), Etihad (twenty-two), British Airways (eighteen), LATAM (fourteen), Japan Airlines (thirteen), Asiana Airlines (ten), Air Lease Corporation (nine), Virgin Atlantic (eight) and Air Caraïbes (three). Subsequently, some of these orders were cancelled, added to, or converted to orders for the A350-900. For example, United Airlines converted its order for thirty-five A350-1000s, originally placed in 2010 and added to in 2013, to forty-five A350-900s in 2017, and has delayed delivery of the first aircraft until 2030.

2023 was the strongest year to date for A350-1000 orders. A total of 134 aircraft were ordered (net 118 aircraft), including significant orders from Air India (thirty-four), Qatar Airways (twenty-three), Eva Air (eighteen), Turkish Airlines (fifteen), Qantas (twelve), Air France (eleven), Lufthansa (ten) and Philippine Airlines (nine). Orders placed during 2024 included Delta Air Lines, for twenty aircraft with options for twenty more, Korean Air, for twenty-seven aircraft as part of its fleet modernisation strategy, and Air India, for another five aircraft. As of 31 July 2025, a total of 354 orders for the A350-1000 had been received by Airbus, of which ninety-eight aircraft had been delivered.

Launch customer Qatar Airways is currently the largest operator of the A350-1000, having twenty-five aircraft with another seventeen still to be delivered. Qatar Airways placed its first order for twenty A350-1000s in June 2007 as part of a large deal, worth $16 billion, for eighty A350s across all variants. The initial order included twenty A350-800s, which were converted to a further seventeen A350-1000s (and three A350-900s) in December 2012 following a decision to focus on the larger A350 variants as they were better suited to the airline's business model. Qatar Airways built up a fleet of nineteen A350-1000s between February 2018 and the end of December 2020. The twentieth aircraft (A7-ANT) was delivered after a hiatus of almost two and a half years owing to legal action over the paint degradation issue described in Chapter 3.

Qatar's A350-1000s carry 327 passengers in a standard two-class configuration, with forty-six Business Class (Qsuite) flat bed seats in a 1-2-1 arrangement and 281 Economy Class standard seats in a 3-3-3 arrangement. During 2023 the carrier introduced a high-density configuration on some of its high-yield demand routes, including Doha to Denpasar, Frankfurt, Johannesburg, Manchester and Seoul; the configuration features 395 seats, of which twenty-four are Business Class and 371 are Economy Class seats. The high density A350-1000 will gradually replace Qatar's 412-seater Boeing 777-300ERs.

British Airways took delivery its first A350-1000 (G-XWBA) in July 2019. It currently operates eighteen aircraft, having received the final aircraft (G-XWBS) on 21 February 2024. Through its parent company, International Airlines Group, British Airways had ordered eighteen A350-1000s, plus eighteen options, in April 2013 as a potential replacement for its older Boeing 767 fleet. The carrier uses a three-class seating layout comprising fifty-six Club Suites, fifty-six World Traveller Plus seats, and 219 World Traveller seats. The Club Suites are a new Business Class product, first launched on the A350, offering direct-aisle access and a privacy door for each seat, which contains high speed wi-fi, a PC power port and an 18.5-in in-flight entertainment screen and the capacity to convert the seat into a flat bed, all in a 1-2-1 arrangement. The World Traveller Plus seats provide passengers with a high level of comfort and amenities in a 2-4-2 arrangement, while the World Traveller seats are ergonomically designed to maximise space and comfort in a 3-3-3 arrangement. British Airways uses its A350-1000 fleet on a wide range of long-haul routes, including London Heathrow to Las Vegas, Cape Town and Mumbai.

Cathay Pacific Airways is currently the joint second largest operator of the A350-1000, also operating eighteen aircraft, and the second airline to introduce the A350-1000 into commercial service after Qatar Airways. Cathay Pacific initially ordered the A350-1000 in August 2012, converting sixteen of a previous order for A350-900 aircraft into the larger variant, and exercising an option to purchase an additional ten A350-1000 aircraft. In September 2017 it converted six orders back to the A350-900. Cathay Pacific received its first A350-1000 (registered as B-LXA) in June 2018 and flew it from Toulouse to Cathay's base in Hong Kong on a blend of biofuel. All eighteen of Cathay Pacific's aircraft have 334 seats: forty-six seats in Business Class (1-2-1 arrangement), thirty-two in Premium Economy (2-4-2 arrangement) and 256 in Standard Economy (3-3-3 arrangement). Cathay Pacific initially operated the A350-1000 on regional services as part of crew familiarisation, beginning with its busiest route – Hong Kong to Taipei – on 1 July 2018. The A350-1000 continues to be used on busy services within the Asia-Pacific region due to its high capacity, as well as on some of the longest routes in Cathay Pacific's network, including Hong Kong to New York JFK, Toronto, Boston, London Heathrow, Manchester, Amsterdam, Madrid and Zurich. Cathay Pacific became the first airline to use the A350-1000 on commercial services to New Zealand in December 2019.

The first production A350-1041 was delivered to launch customer Qatar Airways on 20 February 2018 and registered as A7-ANA. It is shown here flying with one of Qatar Airways' A350-941s (A7-ALY). (Philippe Masclet/Airbus)

A350-1041 A7-ANN of Qatar Airways at London Heathrow Airport. (Anna Zvereva, CC BY-SA 2.0)

British Airways currently operates a fleet of eighteen A350-1041s. G-XWBH is shown on final approach to London Heathrow Airport. (British Airways)

A350-1041 G-XWBE was delivered to British Airways in February 2020. (Colin Cooke, CC BY-SA 2.0)

The flight deck of a British Airways Airbus A350-1041. (Stuart Bailey/British Airways)

The World Traveller cabin of a British Airways A350-1041. (British Airways)

Above: Cathay Pacific Airways is currently the joint second largest operator of the A350-1041 with eighteen aircraft. A350-1041 B-LXD is pictured climbing out from Hong Kong International Airport. (N509FZ, CC BY-SA 4.0)

Below: A350-1041 B-LXO was delivered to Cathay Pacific Airways in March 2021. (Author's collection)

Business Class seating in Cathay Pacific's A350-1041. (Cathay Pacific)

UK carrier Virgin Atlantic announced a $4.4 billion order for twelve A350s in July 2016 as part of a fleet modernisation programme. Eight aircraft were to be purchased by the airline and four were to be acquired on long-term leases from Air Lease Corporation (ALC). Virgin took delivery of its first four A350-1000s in August/September 2019 and began commercial services on 18 September, flying from London Heathrow to New York JFK. The fifth aircraft to join the fleet in September 2020 was a former test aircraft MSN071 (F-WWXL), which was re-registered as G-VDOT. In December 2021 Virgin Atlantic signed an agreement with ALC for the long-term lease of two more A350-1000s, which would eventually increase its fleet to fourteen aircraft. However, Virgin Atlantic has only taken delivery of six A350-1000s from its original order with Airbus for eight examples. In September 2024 it emerged that the airline had cancelled the remaining two A350-1000s following an order for seven Airbus A330-900 aircraft.

Virgin Atlantic currently operates all twelve A350-1000s in its fleet on its long-haul services from London Heathrow, including to Los Angeles, San Francisco, New York JFK, Delhi, Lagos and Orlando, as well as from Manchester to Orlando and Las Vegas, and from Edinburgh to Orlando. Virgin's A350-1000s have compensated for the lost capacity following the COVID-induced early retirement of its remaining Boeing 747 and Airbus A340-600 aircraft.

Virgin Atlantic carries up to 335 passengers on its A350-1000s, dividing the cabin up into a three-class configuration: forty-four Upper Class suites, each seat with a fully lay-flat bed

(1-2-1 arrangement), fifty-six Premium seats (2-4-2 arrangement) and 235 Economy seats (3-3-3 arrangement). The carrier also introduced 'the Loft' and 'the Booth' in its completely redesigned Upper Class cabin. The Loft, which is available on seven of its A350 aircraft, is a social space where passengers can have a drink or dine with friends, or watch a 32-in TV, while the Booth (available on four A350 aircraft) is a luxurious space for two persons to relax and enjoy a drink, a meal or just a change of scene. During 2022 Virgin Atlantic introduced a second (397-seat) configuration on some of its A350-1000s used for flights to leisure destinations such as Orlando and Barbados. It comprises sixteen Upper Class suites (1-2-1 arrangement), fifty-six Premium seats (2-4-2 arrangement) and 325 Economy seats (3-3-3 arrangement), of which forty-five are Economy Delight, providing extra legroom as well as advanced seat selection and priority boarding.

Etihad Airways placed an initial order for twenty-five A350-1000s, plus twenty-five options, in 2008, to be delivered in 2014. However, an announcement of delays in the roll-out and delivery of the A350 caused Etihad to cancel six aircraft from the original firm order in January 2011, and an additional seven in April 2012. At the

Virgin Atlantic A350-1041 G-VLUX on final approach to New York John F. Kennedy Airport, USA. (Adam Moreira, CC BY-SA 4.0)

Above: UK carrier Virgin Atlantic currently operates twelve A350-1041s. G-VBOB, pictured here at Manchester Airport, was delivered in May 2023. (Author's collection)

Below: A350-1041 A6-XWB of Etihad Airways painted in 'Year of the Fiftieth' special colour scheme. (Mark Bess, CC BY-SA 2.0)

The first of seven A350-1041s to enter service with Etihad Airways was A6-XWA in late March 2022. (Anna Zvereva, CC BY-SA 2.0)

Dubai Airshow in November 2013, the carrier reaffirmed an order for ten A350-1000s as part of an overall order for fifty A350s. Financial problems in 2019, resulting in Etihad reducing its route network, flight frequencies and worldwide operations, led to a 92 per cent reduction in its total A350 order to just five A350-1000s, subject to further negotiations. Etihad delayed delivery of its first A350s in late 2019 for strategic reasons, and there were further delays due to the outbreak of the Covid-19 pandemic the following year. Etihad finally introduced its first A350-1000 into service at the end of March 2022 and currently operates seven aircraft featuring Etihad's newest cabin interior: forty-four Business Studios in a 1-2-1 arrangement in the Business Class cabin, each with sliding doors for privacy and forward-facing seats which convert into a flat bed, together with an Economy Class cabin containing 327 seats in a 3-3-3 arrangement, of which forty-five are 'economy space' seats with additional legroom. Etihad operates the A350 on its long-haul routes from Abu Dhabi, including Chicago, Delhi, London Heathrow, Mumbai and New York JFK.

Japan Airlines (JAL) has taken delivery of ten A350-1000s from the thirteen ordered in October 2013 as part of modernisation of its long-haul fleet, the first of which arrived in December 2023. JAL's A350-1000s are gradually replacing its ageing Boeing 777-300ERs, with full delivery expected to be completed by 2028. The A350-1000s are configured to carry up to 239 passengers in four classes: First Class features six suites in a 1-1-1 arrangement, offering a seat and single bed or double bed, Business Class has fifty-four seats in a 1-2-1 arrangement with privacy doors, Premium Economy has twenty-four seats in a 2-4-2 arrangement and Economy Class has 155 seats in a 3-3-3 arrangement. The A350-1000s have initially been put into commercial service on JAL's Tokyo to New York JFK and Dallas routes.

The first A350-1000 for an African carrier was delivered to Ethiopian Airlines on 5 November 2024. It represented the first of four examples ordered by Ethiopian in 2022, each of which will carry up to 395 passengers in a two-class configuration comprising forty-six Business Class and 349 Economy seats. Ethiopian's A350-1000 fleet had grown to four aircraft by the beginning of August 2025.

Other current operators of the A350-1000 are French airlines Air Caraïbes and French Bee. Air Caraïbes operates four A350-1000s on routes from Paris Orly to the French Caribbean. The aircraft are configured to carry 429 passengers in a three-class layout including twenty-four seats in a 2-2-2 arrangement in 'Madras' Business, forty-five seats in a 2-3-2 arrangement in 'Caraïbes' Premium Economy and 360 seats in a high density 3-4-3 arrangement in 'Soleil' Economy'. Air Caraïbes took delivery of its first A350-1000 in December 2019.

French Bee has an all A350 fleet of which two aircraft are A350-1000s, delivered in December 2021 and December 2022, and one aircraft currently on order. Up to 480 passengers are transported on the A350-1000s in a two-class configuration, featuring forty seats in Premium Blue Class (2-4-2 arrangement) and 440 seats in an Eco Blue Class (3-4-3 arrangement), which is sub-divided into three cabin areas. Both A350-1000s routinely fly between Paris Orly and Réunion in the Indian Ocean.

The first A350-1041 to be delivered to Japan Airlines was JA01WJ in December 2023. (Mark Bess, CC BY-SA 2.0)

Japan Airlines' A350-1041, JA02WJ, landing at New York John F. Kennedy Airport, USA. The aircraft is painted with special 'Airbus A350-1000 (Red)' colours. (Mark Bess, CC BY-SA 2.0)

Ethiopian Airlines' A350-1041, ET-BAX, became the second A350-1000 to be operated by Ethiopian after its delivery on 6 December 2024. (Shaun Connor)

Airbus A350-1041s of French airlines Air Caraïbes (F-HSIS) and French Bee (F-HMIX). (Pascal Pigeyre/Airbus)

Air Caraïbes operates four A350-1041s including F-HSIS, shown here landing at Paris Orly Airport, France. (Rémi Dallot)

One of French Bee's two A350-1041s, F-HMIX, landing at Toulouse-Blagnac Airport following a pre-delivery test flight. (Arthur Caudrelier)

Chapter 5

Airbus A350 Enhancements, Other Variants and Potential Developments

Following the development and production of the baseline A350-900 and A350-1000, Airbus has been continually seeking to improve and enhance the efficiency and performance of the aircraft and the passenger experience, and explore opportunities for new variants. This resulting modifications and improvements to the original design have led to the emergence of several additional variants, although not all have come to fruition.

Modifications and Improvements

Airbus is constantly improving existing types to maximise efficiency and meet airline requirements. In 2018, as part of an aerodynamic performance improvement package, Airbus introduced extended winglets together with an adapted span-wise twist of the wing to reduce the induced drag and improve the fuel consumption of the A350-900 by as much as 1 per cent. The package also incorporated structural improvements to lower the empty weight of the aircraft and increase the maximum take-off weight capability to 280 tonnes (617,300 lb) from the initial 268 tonnes of the baseline version. This improvement was initially identified for the A350-900ULR before being made available on the standard A350-900.

In September 2022 Airbus announced plans to transition to a new production standard for the A350-900 and -1000 by 2024. It includes a 1.2-t (2,646-lb) reduction in the structural weight of the aircraft and an increase in the maximum take-off weight by 3 t for the A350-900 to 283 t (623,908 lb) and initially by 2.5 t for the A350-1000 to 319 t (703,275 lb). In October 2023 Airbus revised the increase in the maximum take-off weight for the A350-1000 to 322 t (710,000lb). The new standard allows both variants to maintain their maximum range capability beyond 8,000 nm with an increased payload. The structural weight reductions were achieved through the optimisation and technological improvement of certain systems, structures and installations in different parts of the aircraft, such as the electrical system through new cable concepts, the cabin system by adding a single water tank, a new waste tank and lighter floor panel heating, and the mechanical system through the introduction of new composite air conditioning ducts for improved air circulation. In addition, advanced materials and carbon fibre composites have been used on more parts of the aircraft, including the upper and lower wing covers, door surrounds and the landing gear support structure.

The take-off performance of the A350 has been enhanced through changes to the software responsible for regulating the slat and flap position, which is beneficial for operations at challenging airports, especially those with hot and high-altitude conditions and short runways. A faster landing gear retraction cycle has also been introduced, which contributes to a reduction in aerodynamic drag and greater obstacle clearance.

The 2022 improvements include a 4-in increase in the width of the interior cabin at armrest level, which was achieved by resculpting the cabin sidewalls. In addition, the repositioning of internal features, such as a slight forward shift of the cockpit wall and rearwards move of the rear pressure bulkhead, together with modifications to the arrangement of the forward crew rest area and forward cabin monuments, has allowed 35-in of cabin length to be gained. The extra space can be used to accommodate an additional thirty seats in a typical three-class configuration, with wider seats in the Premium Economy section (19-in seats with a 5-in centre console and an 18-in aisle), a Standard Economy section that could be sold as economy-plus (18.7-in seats in a 3-3-3 configuration) and high-density Economy section (17-in seats in a 3-4-3 configuration) and/or larger galleys and additional lavatories. Cabin enhancements also include the latest generation electro-dimmable windows, which block almost 100 per cent of visible light and infra-red energy and contribute to keeping the cabin interior cooler and improving passenger comfort.

Other Variants

A350 Regional
Airbus considered developing an A350-900 Regional variant in response to the launch of the Boeing 787-10 in June 2013, another variant of the Dreamliner primarily developed for regional, high-demand routes providing more seats but less range. The Regional variant was to be structurally identical to the baseline A350-900 but feature a lower maximum take-off weight of 250 t (551,000 lb) and a reduced maximum engine thrust of 70,000–75,000 lb. It was to be optimised for routes up to 6,800 nm (12,600 km), with seating for up to 360 passengers in a single-class configuration. It was envisaged that the variant would be mainly used for intra-Asian, Middle East to Europe and transatlantic routes with an existing high passenger demand. Singapore Airlines signed up as the launch customer for the regional version in July 2013 and this was followed by an order from Etihad Airways. However, there was no public communication about the variant after 2013 and it was never introduced into service by either airline.

There have been several introductions of 'regional' A350s since 2018, although none have been designated as the A350 Regional variant. Singapore Airlines introduced into service a fleet of regional A350s, which the carrier identified as the A350-900 Medium Haul. The aircraft was specifically configured for regional routes with seating for 303 passengers in a two-class layout (the highest seating capacity among Singapore's A350 fleet), a lower certified maximum weight compared to other A350-900s and at least fourteen examples have de-rated Trent XWB-75 engines.

In 2019, Japan Airlines took delivery of its first A350-900, which was intended for busy domestic routes. It featured 369 seats and had a maximum take-off weight of 217 tonnes (478,500 lb) but was fitted with standard Trent XWB-84 engines.

ACJ350

Airbus Corporate Jets (ACJ) offers the ACJ350 VIP jet. It is a derivative of the A350-900ULR, with an extended range of 11,100 nm (20,550 km) as a result of the increased fuel capacity, and is typically configured for twenty-five passengers. The Luftwaffe (German Air Force) was the first customer to use the ACJ350. It has three aircraft which are intended for political-parliamentary operations by the German government. After delivery, the ACJ350s underwent extensive interior outfitting of a full VIP cabin suite by Lufthansa Technik to make them suitable for use as VIP transport aircraft for government officials, dignitaries, accompanying delegates and invited guests. Up to 120 people can be accommodated. The aircraft are also fitted with high-level communications and radar technology and specific defensive systems.

The first Airbus ACJ350 to be delivered to the Luftwaffe (German Air Force) in August 2020 and registered 10+03. (Bengt Lange/Airbus)

Above: The Luftwaffe has three ACJ350s which are used as VIP transport aircraft for German government officials, dignitaries and accompanying delegates. (Bengt Lange/Airbus)

Below: The first A350-900ULR takes to the air for the first time from Toulouse-Blagnac Airport on 23 April 2018. (Pascal Pigeyre/Airbus)

Singapore Airlines is currently the only operator of the A350-900ULR variant. It has seven examples, including 9V-SGB pictured here. (Mark Bess, CC BY-SA 2.0)

A350-900ULR (Ultra-Long Range)
Airbus launched the A350-900 ultra-long-range programme in October 2015 in response to a firm order from Singapore Airlines for the conversion of seven standard A350-900s, specifically for the carrier's ultra long-haul flights. The A350-900ULR has a maximum take-off weight of 280 t (617,294 lb) and nearly 26,000 litres of additional fuel capacity (166,490 litres compared to 140,795 litres for the standard A350-900). It also features the aerodynamic performance improvement package released in 2018, including extended winglets. The extra fuel capacity has been made available by the relocation of sensors and modifications to the piping and valves in the fuel system rather than through additional fuel tanks. It gives the A350-900ULR a range of 9,700 nm (17,964 km) and flight times of up to twenty hours. However, the extended range can only be attained when the aircraft is operated in a low-density configuration. For example, Singapore Airlines A350-900ULRs have only 161 seats in a two-class configuration.

The first A350-900ULR was rolled out without engines in February 2018 for ground testing. It made its first flight on 23 April 2018. Singapore Airlines received its first -900ULR (9V-SGE) on 14 November 2018 and is currently the only operator of the variant. It is used on some of the longest flights in the world, such as Singapore to New York JFK.

A350-1000F (A350F)
A freighter variant (A350F) of the A350-900 was initially mooted by Airbus in 2007, but it wasn't until July 2021 that the Airbus Board approved a freighter development. The new aircraft is based on the A350-1000, retaining a similar maximum take-off weight of 319 t (703,400 lb), although the fuselage is 10 ft 5 in (3.18 m) shorter in length (total length of 226 ft 7 in / 69.07 m).

It has a main deck cargo door on the left-hand side of the aircraft, just behind the wing, with an opening width of 165 in (4.2 m), making it the largest side door of any freighter. The main deck is reinforced with aluminium floor beams. The lower cargo deck has forward and aft doors on the right-hand side of the fuselage. The A350F has a maximum structural payload of 111 t (244,713 lb) and can carry thirty pallets (96 in × 125 in) or thirty AM-base containers on the main cargo deck and forty LD3 containers or twelve standard pallets on the lower cargo deck.

On completion, the inside of the freighter will be fitted with an optimised and modern full-length cargo loading system to handle both containers and pallets. The sidewalls will be reinforced with a windowless lining while at the front, a 9G cargo barrier wall will separate the flight deck and dedicated flight crew rest area from the main cargo deck. The range of the A350F is estimated to be 4,700 nm (8,700 km) at a 109-t payload.

By the end of March 2025 the freighter had gained sixty-five orders from eleven airlines and lessors, including Turkish Airlines (five), Cathay Pacific (six), Singapore Airlines (seven), Etihad Airways (seven), Air France (four), Martinair (three), Starlux Airlines (ten) and Silk Way West Airlines (two). The entry into service date was initially scheduled for 2026 but due to supply chain challenges it has been delayed until the second half of 2027.

A350-1000ULR and Project Sunrise

Project Sunrise is the name given to Qantas' plans for direct non-stop flights from Sydney and Melbourne to London Heathrow and New York JFK. The 'Sunrise' routes will be the longest non-stop commercial flights in the world: 9,200 nm (17,020 km) and a flight time of over nineteen hours.

The A350 has been selected by Qantas as its preferred choice for Project Sunrise and Airbus is working on an A350-1000ULR for the programme. It will have a 20,000-litre centre fuel tank fitted within the wing box, giving the aircraft a range of 9,700 nm (18,000 km) and the possibility of 22-hour-long flights. Qantas initially ordered twelve aircraft in 2022 and a further twelve in 2023, with deliveries due to begin in mid-2026. The A350-1000ULR will accommodate 238 passengers in a four-class configuration, including First suites, Business suites, Premium Economy and Economy seating. It will also feature a dedicated 'Wellbeing

Created image of the Airbus A350F freighter variant of the A350-1000. (Airbus)

Zone', which will be a space available to all passengers where they can follow specially guided programmes on large monitors promoting movement and stretching and consume a selection of healthy refreshments to ensure hydration.

In May 2023, Philippine Airlines signed a Memorandum of Understanding to purchase nine A350-1000ULRs for the operation of non-stop services from Manila to the east coast of the USA and Canada.

Above: Scale model of the A350F on display at the 2024 Farnborough Airshow. (Hervé Goussé/Airbus)

Below: Created image of the A350-1000ULR, which has been selected for Qantas' Project Sunrise. (Airbus)

Passenger cabin of Qantas' Project Sunrise A350-1000ULR. (Qantas)

Potential Developments

In 2016 Airbus explored a possible stretched version of the A350-1000 with a select group of airlines. The potential new variant featured a 4-m extension of the fuselage to provide an additional forty-five seats, which would result in a capacity of 400–440 seats in a typical two-class configuration. The increased seating capacity would remain within the permitted emergency exit limits of four doors on each side of the aircraft, so no additional safety exits would be required. The maximum take-off weight was estimated to be 319 t and the aircraft was to be powered by Trent XWB-97 engines. It was internally designated A350-2000 (also A350-1100 and A350-8000 have been suggested) and would have a range of 7,600 nm (14,100 km). Despite a marginally lower passenger capacity than the Boeing 777-9, it was considered to be a very competitive alternative, having a lower maximum take-off and empty weight resulting in a significantly more cost efficient aircraft. However, the 'A350 stretch' proposal was not progressed, possibly due to the potential impact on the demand for the A380 and A350-1000, and the programme was shelved in 2017 due to the lack of market appeal.

There remains a possibility that a stretched A350-1000 could be re-evaluated in the future, given sufficient customer interest and market demand, which may be stimulated by the need to replace progressively aging fleets and a new generation of turbofan powerplants. Ultra-high bypass ratio engine developments are currently being explored by Rolls-Royce through its UltraFan programme, Pratt & Whitney's upgrade of its PW1000G family and by Safran Aircraft Engines, working in parallel with its partner, General Electric.

The future availability of a new generation of engines could also lead to the development of an A350neo ('new engine option') in the early 2030s, potentially to compete with a Boeing New Midsize Aircraft, should Boeing recommence its development.

Appendix

Airbus A350 Technical Specifications

	Airbus A350-941	Airbus A350-1041
Length	66.80 m (219 ft 2 in)	73.79 m (242 ft 1 in)
Height	17.05 m (55 ft 11 in)	17.08 m (56 ft 0 in)
Fuselage width	5.96 m (19 ft 7 in)	
Wingspan	64.75 m (212 ft 5 in)	
Wing area	442 m² (4,758 sq ft)	464.3 m² (4,998 sq ft)
Wing sweep	31.9 degrees	
Cabin length	51.04 m (167 ft 5 in)	58.03 m (190 ft 5 in)
Cabin width	5.61 m/5.71 m (18 ft 5 in/18 ft 9 in)	
Typical seating in a three-class configuration	300–350 (315 in two-class configuration)	350–410 (369 in two-class configuration)
Maximum seating	440	480
Lower-deck cargo	36 LD3 containers or 11 pallets	44 LD3 containers or 14 pallets
Zero fuel weight	195.70 t	223.00 t
Max take-off weight	283.00 t (623,908 lb)	322.00 t (710,000 lb)
Max landing weight	207.00 t	236.00 t
Max fuel capacity	140,795–166,490 l (ULR)	158,791–164,000 l
Max payload	53.3 t (118,000 lb)	67.3 t (148,000 lb)
Cruise speed	Typical: Mach 0.85 (488 kn; 903 km/h; 561 mph) Max: Mach 0.89 (513 kn; 950 km/h; 591 mph)	
Range	15,742 km (8,500 nm) 17,964 km (9,700 nm) (ULR)	16,482 km (8,900 nm)
Engines (x2)	Rolls-Royce Trent XWB-84	Rolls-Royce Trent XWB-97
Composition of the airframe	Carbon fibre-reinforced polymer (CFRP): 53% Advanced aluminium alloys: 19% Titanium: 14% Steel: 6% Other materials: 8%	

(Source: airbus.com)